Justice for Women?

Family, court and social control

Mary Eaton

St Mary's College, Strawberry Hill

Open University Press
Milton Keynes · Philadelphia

Open University Press
Open University Educational Enterprises Limited
12 Cofferidge Close
Stony Stratford
Milton Keynes MK11 1BY, England

and
242 Cherry Street
Philadelphia, PA 19106, USA

First published 1986

British Library Cataloguing in Publication Data

Eaton, Mary
  Justice for women? family, court and
  social control.
  1. Defence (Criminal procedure)—England
  2. Women—England   3. Police magistrates
  —England   4. Criminal justice,
  Administration of—England
  I. Title
  344.205'7   KD8309

  ISBN 0-335-15351-8
  ISBN 0-335-15350-X Pbk

Library of Congress Cataloging in Publication Data

Eaton, Mary.
  Justice for women?
  Includes index.
  1. Justices of the peace—Great Britain.
  2. Judicial process—Great Britain.   3. Female offenders
  —Great Britain.   4. Sex discrimination in criminal
  justice administration—Great Britain.   I. Title.
  KD8309.E28 1987   347.41'05'024041   86-8538

  ISBN 0-335-15350-X (pbk.)   344.1075024041
  ISBN 0-335-15351-8

Text design by Carlton Hill
Typeset by Rowland Phototypesetting Ltd,
Bury St Edmunds, Suffolk.
Printed in Great Britain by
J. W. Arrowsmith,
in Bristol

For my mother and my father

Contents

List of Tables

Acknowledgements

I would like to thank:

the police officers, probation officers, magistrates and court personnel at 'Hillbury' who assisted me in many ways, and particularly the Clerk to the Justices and the Chief Probation Officer who proved to be the most facilitating of gatekeepers;

Professor Terence Morris of the LSE who with his customary care and attention supervised the Ph.D. thesis on which this book is based;

St Mary's College, Strawberry Hill for time free from teaching in which to conduct the research and for encouragement in the completion of the work;

those who provided valuable comment and criticism at various stages – Carole Bourne, Julia Brophy, Maureen Cain, Peter Hammond, Paul Rock and especially those who read the first draft of the manuscript and who in discussing the work with me, contributed much to its development – Frances Heidensohn, Christopher Knee, Jeremy Roche, and Carol Smart;

and Liz Francis who patiently and skilfully typed it all.

Material in Chapter 5 originally appeared in an article in Julia Brophy and Carol Smart (eds) *Women-In-Law*, Routledge & Kegan Paul, 1985. I am grateful to the publisher for permission to reproduce it. I am also grateful to the author and publisher for enabling me to read Frances Heidensohn *Women and Crime*, Macmillan, 1985, prior to publication.

. . . I know nothing like the petty grinding tyranny of a good English family. And the only alleviation is that the tyrannized submits with a heart full of affection.

Florence Nightingale's diary (1851)

My mother has just come into my room . . . She . . . started mumbling on about 'adult relationships' and life being complicated' and how she must 'find herself . . .' And then she said that for some women marriage is like being in prison. Then she went out.

Marriage is nothing like being in prison! Women are let out every day to go to the shops and stuff, and quite a lot go to work. I think my mother is being a bit melodramatic.

The Secret Diary of Adrian Mole aged 13¾ Sue Townsend (1982)

Chapter One

Justice, crime and social control

This book is primarily about women and magistrates' courts, but I hope it
will have a relevance beyond the criminal justice system. In describing
how the routine processes of summary justice reinforce the social position
of women my concern is not only with the minority of women who appear
before the court, but also with the majority of women who are never
involved, personally, with the formal agents of law enforcement. These
women, too, are affected by the model of family life which dominates the
discourse of the magistrates' court. This model is to be found in discussions
in parliamentary committees and boardrooms, in classrooms and work-
shops, and throughout the mass media. Constant and continued use
strengthens the ideological dominance of this model which, within the
magistrates' courts and beyond, structures the perceived reality of
women's lives. We need to become aware of the subtle operation of this
model in specific situations if we are to understand the reproduction of the
subordination of women. One such specific situation is a magistrates' court
on the edge of London – a small part of the state apparatus expressly
concerned with justice. It is here that my work begins, but it is rooted
within a tradition of feminist study.

Women and sociology

In the early 1970s, feminists once again began to turn their attention to areas of their lives in which they and other women had experienced oppression or denial. For many sociologists this resulted in an awareness that a subject which claimed to explore and analyse society was dealing mainly with men and men's experiences. Some responded by urging that women's perspectives and experiences be examined in order to redress the balance. Others argued that the paucity of women in sociological studies was due to more than oversight or misogyny on the part of researchers and writers, and had much to do with the construction of sociology as a discipline. This point is made by Ann Oakley who claims that to try to fit women into categories previously occupied chiefly by men is to wrongly assume that such categories are neutral.

> The broad subject divisions current in modern sociology appear, at first sight, to be eminently logical and non-sexist. Social stratification, political institutions, religion, education, deviance, the sociology of industry and work, the family and marriage, and so on: these are, surely, just descriptions of different areas of human social life. (Oakley, 1974:4)

Oakley questions whether these categories are useful in studying the social reality of most women.[1]

> ... to what extent are the experiences of women *actually* represented in the study of these life-areas; and how does the representation compare with the empirical role of women in social life; ... do the subject categorisations *themselves* make sense from the perspective of women's particular situation. (Ibid, Original emphasis)

Bearing in mind Oakley's critique of sociology it is interesting to see how recent work has approached the problem of studying women within the pre-existing category of 'deviance'.

Women and deviance

Writing in 1968, Frances Heidensohn drew attention to:

> ... an obscure and largely ignored area of human behaviour, namely deviance in women. (Heidensohn, 1968:160)

She argued that such obscurity was inappropriate to a topic that should be of interest to sociologists who since Durkheim had been concerned with crime and deviance as a subject matter. However, since women criminals, by their number, do not pose a serious social problem, they had been generally disregarded as a sociological problem. Dominant criminological theories were based on men, and little attention had been paid to either the deviance (including crime) or the apparent conformity of women. Heidensohn called for:

> . . . a crash programme of research which telescopes decades of comparable studies of males. (Heidensohn, 1968:171)

In the USA Dorie Klein (1973) produced a polemical critique of the current criminological work on women. Like Heidensohn, she lamented the lack of attention that had been given to the subject by all but a small group of theorists. She then proceeded to analyse the contribution made by these theorists, all of whom had certain features in common:

> The writers see criminality as the result of *individual* characteristics that are only peripherally affected by economic, social and political forces. These characteristics are of a *physiological* or *psychological* nature and are uniformly based on implicit or explicit assumptions about the *inherent nature of women*. This nature is *universal*, rather than existing within a specific historical framework. (Klein, 1973:58, Original emphasis.)

Such concentration on the individual poses the problem, and the solution, as one of individual adjustment rather than social change. Klein sees these theorists to be concerned with the good order of the *status quo* rather than the welfare of the women within that social structure. Female criminality had been explained by female biology and female psychology which accounted for the acceptable behaviour of the 'good' woman and the 'unacceptable' behaviour of the bad woman. By linking behaviour to 'nature' such theorists ignored the social construction of gender roles. The issue had been raised and the response began.

With hindsight it is possible to recognise three more or less distinct strands in the resulting publications:

(i) *Redressing the balance*

The first, coming mainly from the USA, consisted of work which might be seen as a response to Heidensohn's call for a 'crash programme of research'. These are studies of women's crime, women criminals and the treatment of women by the criminal justice system, (e.g. Simon, 1977; Adler and Simon, 1979; Datesman and Scarpitti, 1980; Warren, 1981). Such texts are attempts to redress the balance by producing work on women to mirror the traditional criminological work on men. This work deals with a minority of women, and usually does so in a way which emphasises the difference between deviant and non-deviant women. There are few attempts to relate the situations and experiences of this minority to the wider population of women, and the result is interesting accounts, but ones which usually appear irrelevant to the lives of the majority of women.

(ii) *Liberation leads to Crime*

The second strand consists of those writers who were not prepared to accept that only a minority of women become involved in crime. They argued that as equal rights legislation gave women more opportunities this was being reflected in a greater involvement in the world of crime (Adler, 1975). This argument is based on a percentage increase, rather than a significant rise in the number of crimes committed by women. Since the actual number of recorded crimes by women in low, a small numerical increase means a large percentage increase in relation to the number of crimes recorded for previous years. In relation to men, women remain responsible for a small proportion of the total crime. Furthermore, the 'liberation leads to crime' thesis overestimated the effects of legislation on the lives of the majority of women. Few women actually experienced a significant improvement in their social position as the result of equal rights legislation, and the women who come before the courts are usually those least affected by the ideas or the material benefits of women's liberation. Nevertheless the thesis proved popular in the mass media, probably because it corresponded with dominant attitudes to the appropriate social control of women. In a careful appraisal of the literature on this debate, Box and Hale (1983) conclude that there is no substance in this argument based, chiefly, on speculation and a mis-reading of official statistics.

(iii) *Beyond criminology*

Neither of the two approaches considered so far is very helpful in achieving a fuller understanding of the relationship of criminal and deviant women to the wider society, the first approach is limited, the second is misguided. However, a third, more fruitful approach developed and it is this which has most influenced my work. This tradition grew within the perspective of feminist work and in recognition of the limitations of criminology – including the radical criminology which was developing during the early 1970s.

This radical, or 'new' criminology is most clearly defined by *The New Criminology* published in 1973. In this book the authors, Taylor, Walton and Young critique the prevailing ideologies and unexplicated assumptions which they saw in traditional criminology; their aim was to produce 'a fully social theory of deviance', one which set the actors in their social and political context. However, while the authors discussed the class bias of much existing work on crime and deviance, they failed to recognise the sexism which had led to a neglect and distortion of female criminality and deviance. Work which claimed to present a radical departure was, in fact, reproducing the old sexist bias. This did not go unnoticed.

In 1976, Carol Smart published *Women, Crime and Criminology* which supplied a critique of the sexism which she recognised as permeating both sociological and non-sociological accounts of crime and deviance by women and girls. However, as she herself recognised, such criticism may be necessary but it is not sufficient.

> Critique is a prerequisite for the formulation of an alternative perspective. (Smart, 1976:xv)

What was needed was an approach which could adequately encompass and represent the lives of women and girls rather than an attempt to supply a female component to pre-existing, male dominated, sociological categories. As Oakley and other feminists had argued, it was necessary to take the actual lives of women as the starting point, and if these evaded or confused existing sociological categories then it was the categories that needed reshaping or reconceptualising. If women and girls did not appear in many studies of crime and delinquency, because of their under-representation in these areas, then it was necessary to look not just at the few who became publicly labelled 'deviant', but at the many who did not, and at those whose 'deviance' label related to areas other than crime (e.g. health). It was necessary to abandon the rigidity of the category of 'rule-breaker' in order to study those who break rules *and* those who conform, and to discuss the relationship between such groups of women.

This was the perspective adopted by two collections of articles on women and deviance which appeared in 1978 and 1981. *Women, Sexuality and Social Control* (Smart and Smart, 1978) contains papers which deal with traditional criminological concerns like prostitution (McIntosh) and juvenile delinquency (Shacklady-Smith) as well a papers which deal with non-judicial areas of social control such as doctor–patient interaction (Barrett and Roberts) and the position of wives within marital households (Dahl and Snare). Overt and covert forms of control are discussed in relation to deviancy and conformity, while the phenomena under discussion are analysed not by reference to individual pathologies, but in relation to the social structure.

A similar concern to examine deviant and non-deviant behaviours, together with judicial and non-judicial forms of social control, is expressed in *Controlling Women: The Normal and The Deviant* (Hutter and Williams, 1981). Here papers on prostitution (Smart; McLeod), prison (Rowett and Vaughan) and alcoholism (Otto) are presented with papers on motherhood (Oakley) and old age (Evers; Phillipson). The editors use this juxtaposition of 'deviant' and 'normal' to achieve a better understanding of the relationship of women to authority structures.

> Examination of the explicit controls exercised over women who are seen as deviant because they act in ways beyond the bounds of 'normal society' helps us to clarify (the) concept of 'normal behaviour'. Furthermore, it allows us to see more clearly the extent and nature of the covert controls employed to persuade all women to fit their behaviour into this normal pattern. (Hutter and Williams, 1981:9)

In this approach the boundaries between women defined as criminal or deviant, and other women, become obscure. As one recognises that the regulation applied to deviant women is on a continuum of regulation applied to all women, so one is drawn away from discussing deviant women as a separate group and towards discussing the social controls that affect all women. In a thoughtful and perceptive discussion of this approach Frances Heidensohn reviews the literature on women and crime and concludes:

> Ultimately the best way to understand women and crime seemed to be . . . in using the insights into the role, position and social control of women which can be derived from other studies of women's oppression. (Heidensohn, 1985:197)

This shift in perspective, away from traditional criminological orientations, has the potential of a better understanding of women's relationship to crime:

> If we start from the broader issues of conformity and control and observe and analyse how these effect *all* women to *some* degree and some groups of women more than other, we can learn rather more about those who become involved in crime as compared with other kinds of activities which might be available to them. (Ibid; 199, Original emphasis.)

While some writers have extended the categories of deviance and social control to include conformity and both formal and informal controls, others have taken traditional subject areas, but extended the scope of the research beyond the boundaries which usually limit such areas. Recent work on prostitutes and on women prisoners has presented the subjects of the research not as pathological misfits, but as women in a particular situation, one which arises out of a conjunction of their class position and their gender role within a specific location in contemporary Britain (McCleod, 1982; Carlen, 1983).

In *Women Working: Prostitution Now*, Eileen McCleod (1982) presents the lives of her respondents as a response to the economic pressures of child-care and the low wages available to women in alternative employment. Prostitution is seen in the context of a society which assumes that women's wages do not need to support a family despite the fact that many women are solely responsible for the care and maintenance of children. Having interviewed the clients, McCleod discusses the prostitutes–client relationship in the context of gender socialisation. The women and men in this study are depicted as individuals whose problems and responses arise not from individual pathology, but from economic and cultural practices which structure the relations of women and men to the labour market and to the domestic sphere. However, McCleod also moves beyond the lives of her individual subjects to examine the aspects of the wider social structure which directly impinge on their lives, specifically the laws on prostitution and the contradictions contained in the formulation and operation of those laws.

A similar move from the lives of specific women in a particular situation to a discussion of the structures which affect the majority of women, can be found in Pat Carlen's (1983) *Women's Imprisonment*. Here Carlen describes the lives of 20 prisoners and in so doing critiques the processes of surveillance and control, both within and beyond the prison, which limit the options of women already disadvantaged by the ill effects of poverty and alcoholism. She demonstrates how ideologies of family life and the woman's role, together with the organisational practices of medical and social workers, combine to produce a situation in which women who resist the oppression of their gender-role are in danger of becoming subject to the coercion of the penal system. Women who resist the physical violence of a man by attacking him as he sleeps, or women who attempt to nullify the effects of poverty and despair by turning to alcohol, are likely to find themselves facing charges which may lead to prison. An absence of money to pay fines, and administrative difficulties over the making of probation orders in Scotland, reduce the tariff options available to the courts. Those women who place their children in care, rather than subject them to the brutality of life with a violent father, in sub-standard accommodation, are regarded as uncaring mothers. Without the obligation of child-care they can more easily be given a prison sentence. Once in prison the women encounter a system which reproduces the isolation, dependence and vulnerability which characterises the lives of many women within their families. Here at the most severe point of the criminal justice system there is a discouragement of self-reliance and co-operative activity among women. Carlen presents a valuable case study of life within a women's prison, but she also, in describing the experiences of her respondents, presents a critique of ideologies and social practices which leave women, particularly working-class women, vulnerable to violence, poverty and madness. Her case study provides intense instances of the regulation to which all women are subject.

Both McCleod and Carlen use a case study to give a detailed account of a specific situation. However, by situating such accounts in the context of the wider society they are able to provide a critique which has relevance beyond the initial case study. By relating the lives of the individuals in the case study to the wider social structure, they are able to draw out the aspects of that structure which will have an influence in many other situations. The value of the case study lies not only in what it tells us about an unknown or under-researched part of society, but also, and more importantly, in how it relates that part to the whole. Case studies allow us to make a detailed investigation of empirical reality, but if they are more than travellers' tales they will provide a new perspective on, and a better understanding of, other areas of society. In the chapters that follow, I use a case study as a means of achieving a better understanding of the way in which gender differences are reinforced by summary justice in a magistrates' court.

Justice and equality

Despite a decade of equal rights legislation women remain a consistently disadvantaged group in Britain today. The Equal Pay Act 1970 and the Sex Discrimination Act 1975 provided the legal obligation of 'equal treatment', but women remain the poorest members of each class, earning less than men because they tend to be concentrated in jobs that pay less, and working longer hours since paid employment is frequently combined with domestic labour and the care of the young, the sick or the aged. In such a situation questions of 'justice' and 'equality' become problematic. What would constitute 'justice' for women and how is this to be achieved? Is it a fundamental mistake to expect legislation to institute change? What can the courts, with their explicit commitment to 'justice', be expected to do?

For feminists campaigning during the last century and in the early years of this century the law was a clearly recognised area around which to organise their demands. There were legal obstacles, as well as social attitudes and customs, limiting the aims and aspirations of women. On matters relating to family duties and responsibilities, on access to education and jobs, on control over income and property, on political recognition feminists fought to achieve the status of adults, with the same rights as adult men (Sachs and Wilson, 1978; Brophy and Smart, 1985). However, even during this period when legislative reform was clearly necessary, there were debates on the meaning of 'justice' and 'equality' for women. While some argued for equal treatment, others wanted positive discrimination which recognised, and sought to redress, the existing inequalities.

> Some early twentieth-century feminists . . . wanted primarily to focus upon achieving equality with men. However, they came into direct conflict with other women who felt that such a goal was unreasonable in view of women's responsibility for children. For these ('new') feminists (e.g. Eleanor Rathbone, 1912, 1927), a focus upon women's childbearing responsibilities led to a very different analysis of women's position and hence to a quite different political goal. They concentrated upon campaigning for a form of positive discrimination in favour of women. (Brophy and Smart, 1985:5)

The question is still with us. The Equal Pay Act and the Sex Discrimination Act both define 'equality' for women as parity of treatment with men. Both acts employ a concept of justice based on uniform treatment rather than positive discrimination. This concept of 'justice' is also to be found in the criminal justice system. Individual or class differences are not officially recognised by the Law and while many argue that the courts respond favourably to those with wealth and resources (Box, 1971; Griffiths, 1977) there is no provision for explicitly redressing the balance for those who appear before the court already disadvantaged in relation to the rest of society. On the contrary, there is pride in the knowledge that the figure of Justice – the embodiment of the British legal system – standing above the Central Criminal Court in London, is blindfold, and so cannot distinguish between the individuals who come before her.

However, to accept that 'justice' and 'equality' are to be achieved by parity of treatment is to collude in the acceptance of the inequalities which co-exist with such 'equal treatment'. To assume that justice for women means treating women like men is to ignore the very different existences which distinguish the lives of women from the lives of men of similar social status. Yet this attitude to 'justice' and 'equality' not only underlies legislative provision, it is also to be found in studies of the law and the criminal justice system. It was from this perspective that my own study began.

A case study

My work originated as a comparative study of the treatment of the male and female defendants who appeared before one magistrates' court. When the study began, in 1980, this was an area marked more by speculation and discussion than empirical investigation. There were claims that women, compared with men, were treated leniently by the courts, and counter-claims that they were treated harshly. Most of the research which did exist was based on official statistics, focused on juvenile delinquents, and/or had been carried out in the USA. There was little work on adult women defendants in the UK. I decided to focus on the interactions within one magistrates' court, and on the perspectives and practices of those who play a routine part in the social construction of summary justice. The court is referred to as 'Hillbury Court' (a pseudonym). Pseudonyms are also used when referring to defendants.

The traditional question of discrimination was addressed and tested using a number of approaches which tried to hold constant a variety of factors relating to male and female defendants. Previous convictions and present circumstances were considered in relation to requests for social inquiry reports, the construction of social inquiry reports, arguments used in mitigation, and sentencing. By all relevant criteria, it seemed that men and women received similar treatment when they appeared in similar circumstances. And this confirmed the findings of work on a larger scale (Farrington and Morris, 1983). If the issue of sexism within the court is addressed solely in terms of differential treatment then the court can be exonerated.

However, by spending time in court, I had become aware of the ways in which lawyers presented both women and men to the court, and of the responses of the magistrates to such presentations. Specifically, I had become aware of the dominance of a particular model of the family in the pleas of mitigation on behalf of both women and men. This model of the family, is one which ascribes specific gender roles to men and women and which has been the subject of much feminist critique (Land, 1978; McIntosh, 1979; Smart, 1984). The ideological dominance of this model is not matched by its empirical prevalence, nevertheless by the dominance of such a model other forms of household arrangement are marginalised (Smart, 1984:xiii).

The focus of my study changed. Although I still compared the sentences received by men and women, and the other aspects of the judicial procedure in which difference might be manifest, I now concentrated on the language in use in the court, and on the model of the family that such language revealed. This perspective was also applied to social inquiry reports and to the interviews.

From this work I came to an understanding that women are disadvantaged by the court not specifically in relation to men defendants, but more generally in relation to men, within the family and, consequently, throughout society. Women are seen by the court, as they are by other institutions, (e.g. education, labour market, mass media) as primarily home-centred. By its use of the ideologically dominant model of the family the court endorses this model and the gender roles which it entails, it adds its weight to the way women are perceived by other institutions. The prevalence of this view of women makes it unremarkable, almost unnoticeable. Nevertheless, while the continued subordination of women may be manifest most clearly in specific acts of obvious discrimination, it is also revealed and continually reinforced by the way we talk about women and men. Language is the means by which we make sense of the world, and the means by which we communicate that sense to others. Common language use leads to common sense, a shared understanding which is continually reinforced by that language use (Sapir, 1949; Whorf, 1956). Language is, therefore, vital in understanding social reality; it is at the core of our perception of the world and central to our interactions with others.

There is a silence in my work on the issues of ethnic differences and the reproduction of racism. This is, in part, due to the circumstances of the research, which was conducted in a court with very few Black defendants and no Black magistrates, probation officers or lawyers. Of course this does not mean that racism was not present. Certainly the model of family which was dominant in the court is a model associated with the life-style of a white middle-class. There may be many ways in which the situation of Black women and men is reinforced by the routine practices of the court; I was not alert to them and this is a limitation which is shared by many white feminists (Amos and Parmar, 1984; Barrett and McIntosh, 1985). However, the issue of racism within the criminal justice system will, I hope, be addressed in the near future so that we may achieve a fuller understanding of the ways in which this state apparatus reproduces social divisions.[2]

Courts like Hillbury exist all over the country. Anyone may walk into the local court and watch and listen, verify or dispute what I have to say. Although I had access to documents and personnel that would not be available to the casual visitor, I base much of my argument on what took place in open court, and it was those interactions which first alerted me to the dominance of a particular model of the family in courtroom rhetoric.

Chapter Two

Differential sentencing: a limited approach

Traditionally, the issue of sexism in the courts has been addressed by comparing the sentences received by women and men. My own work began in this way, but I soon recognised the limitations of this approach. Much of the work carried out in this area is limited even within the terms of its own methodology, i.e. it does not adequately control for relevant factors when comparing two groups of offenders. However, even the work which is rigorous in the application of this methodology suffers from the limits inherent within this approach, i.e. the focus on sentencing obscures the importance of the judicial process of which the sentence is but the end result, and distorts the significance of factors which appear relevant to the sentence. The best of the work on differential sentencing has a valid contribution to make to the debate on discrimination within the court. However, the debate is conducted within the terms of legal rhetoric – 'justice' and 'equality' mean 'equal treatment', existing inequalities are to be ignored or discounted. Such work is incapable of revealing the subtle and pervasive influences of sexism. While recognising the contribution of the best of these studies, I hope to go further by demonstrating the fruitfulness of understanding the judicial process within the context of the society of which it is a part. To do this I will focus on the way in which the courts make use of gender roles within the family.

Facts, figures and female offenders

The criminality of women and the response of the criminal justice system are subjects which have engendered a growing amount of interest in recent years. For many writers the official statistics are a record of judicial rather than criminal activity, i.e. they record those offenders who have appeared before the courts, and the results of such appearances.

However, these figures show distinctive patterns both in the offences with which women are charged and the sentences they receive. Writing in 1968, Frances Heidensohn commented:

Table 2.1 Offenders found guilty at all courts, by sex and type of offence in England and Wales, 1983 (Source: Home Office (1984) Table 5.1)

Offence	Males		Females	
	Number (thousands)	Percentage	Number (thousands)	Percentage
Indictable Offences				
Violence against the person	47.4	92	4.0	8
Sexual offences	6.4	98	0.1	2
Burglary	70.3	97	2.4	3
Robbery	3.8	95	0.2	5
Theft and handling stolen goods	179.5	80	45.3	20
Fraud and forgery	20.1	79	5.5	21
Criminal damage	11.2	93	0.8	7
Other (excluding motoring)	30.0	90	3.4	10
Motoring	29.6	97	1.0	3
TOTAL	398.4	86	62.7	14
Summary Offences				
Offences (excluding motoring)	390.4	83	82.4	17
Motoring	1,053.7	91	108.1	9
TOTAL	1,444.1	88	190.4	12
All offences	1,842.4	88	253.1	12

... differences between the patterns and manifestations of male and female deviance were long ago observed, they were observed, moreover, to differ with that kind of regularity and uniformity which normally attract the attention of the social scientist. (Heidensohn, 1968:161)

Such patterns have given rise to claims that women are treated leniently by the courts and to counter-claims that they are treated harshly. However, the status of such figures as a resource is questionable. While the patterns are clearly observable there is a danger in mis-reading the information conveyed by these figures. What, then, may we deduce from the criminal statistics?

Firstly, we can conclude that women form a small proportion of all known offenders (see Table 2.1). In only two categories of crime (theft and fraud) do they account for as much as one fifth of the offenders involved. Secondly, we can see that women appear much more restricted than men in their criminal involvements. For indictable offences the highest concentration of all offenders is in the area of theft; however while this accounts for 45 per cent of the men, it accounts for 72 per cent of the women (Table 2.2).

Table 2.2 Distribution of indictable offences between male and female populations of offenders found guilty at all courts in England and Wales, 1983 (Source: Home Office (1984) Table 5.1)

Indictable Offence	Males		Females	
	Number (thousands)	Percentage	Number (thousands)	Percentage
Violence against the person	47.4	12	4.0	6
Sexual offences	6.4	2	0.1	0.2
Burglary	70.3	18	2.4	4
Robbery	3.8	1	0.2	0.3
Theft and handling stolen goods	179.5	45	45.3	72
Fraud and forgery	20.1	5	5.5	9
Criminal damage	11.2	3	0.8	1
Other (excluding motoring)	30.0	8	3.4	5
Motoring	29.6	7	1.0	2
TOTAL	398.4	101*	62.7	99.5

*Percentage figures do not sum to 100 as in most cases they have been rounded up or down to the nearest whole number.

Furthermore, even within the area of theft crimes, women are more concentrated than men. In 1983 shoplifting accounted for 26 per cent of theft offences by men, but 64 per cent of theft offences by women (Table 2.3). However, it is interesting to note that because of the actual numbers involved men accounted for the larger number of shoplifting offences.

The criminal statistics, then, can serve a useful purpose in revealing the noticeable differences in the types of offences for which men and women are sentenced by the courts, and it is important to remember these differences when looking at the distribution of sentences between men and women offenders (Table 2.4).

The official statistics reveal that a high proportion of women offenders receive the less severe sentences. The distribution of sentences between men and women has remained fairly constant over the years; most offenders of both sexes are fined, but a higher proportion of men receive sentences of imprisonment, while a higher proportion of women receive a

Table 2.3 Distribution of theft offences between male and female populations of offenders found guilty at all courts in England and Wales, 1983 (Source: Home Office (1984) Table 5.1)

Offence	Males		Females	
	Number	Percentage	Number	Percentage
Theft from the person of another	1,933	1	352	1
Theft in a dwelling	2,489	1	674	2
Theft by an employee	5,834	3	1,514	3
Theft from mail	245	0.1	32	0.1
Abstracting electricity	2,644	2	984	2
Theft of pedal cycle	3,327	2	72	0.2
Theft from vehicle	11,621	7	181	0.4
Theft from shops	46,018	26	29,189	64
Theft from automatic machine or meter	5,238	3	1,270	3
Theft of motor vehicle	28,753	16	725	2
Other theft	48,537	27	6,472	14
Handling stolen goods	22,895	13	3,853	9
TOTAL	179,534	101.1	45,318	100.7

Table 2.4 Type of sentence or order given to all offenders in England and Wales, 1983 (Source: Home Office (1984) Table 7.3)

Sentence or Order	Males Number (thousands)	Percentage	Females Number (thousands)	Percentage
Absolute or conditional discharge	44.2	11	14.5	23.1
Probation order	24.1	6	9.9	15.6
Supervision order	11.2	2.8	1.6	2.6
Fine	171.7	43	27.6	44
Community service order	29.8	7.5	1.6	2.6
Attendance centre	14.2	3.6	0.5	0.8
Detention centre	11.5	2.8	—	—
Care order	1.8	0.5	0.3	0.5
Borstal training	3.3	0.8	0.1	0.2
Youth custody	11.0	2.8	0.5	0.8
Imprisonment:				
Fully suspended	26.7	6.7	3.2	5.1
Partly suspended	3.5	0.9	0.3	0.5
Unsuspended	41.4	10.4	2.0	3.2
Otherwise	4.9	1.2	0.6	1
TOTAL	399.2	100	62.7	100

probation order or a discharge. The difference is even greater when one considers the fate of offenders over 21 (Table 2.5).

However, before prematurely concluding that these figures demonstrate the leniency of the courts towards women, it is important to remember that a sentence is a response to a specific situation, and that while many aspects of the situation are not recorded in the official statistics those that are recorded point to differences in recorded male and female crime, from which one expects differences in judicial response. Sentencing takes account of not only the type of crime (e.g. theft) but also other factors such as the gravity of the offence (e.g. the value of the goods taken), the circumstances of the offence (e.g. the involvement of others, the role of the defendant) and the previous convictions of the defendant. What we know of these other factors leads us to recognise further differences in the recorded patterns of male and female crime.

Table 2.5 Type of sentence or order given to offenders over 21, in England and Wales, 1983 (Source: Home Office (1984) Tables 7.11, 7.12)

Sentence or Order	Males		Females	
	Number (thousands)	Percentage	Number (thousands)	Percentage
Absolute or conditional discharge	18.4	9	8.6	21
Probation order	13.3	6	6.8	17
Fine	100.8	47	18.6	46
Community service order	14.3	7	1.0	2
Imprisonment:				
Fully suspended	24.6	11	2.9	7
Partly suspended	3.5	2	0.3	1
Unsuspended	38.0	18	1.8	4
Otherwise	3.1	1	0.5	1
TOTAL	216.2	101*	40.5	99*

*Percentage figures do not sum to 100 as they have been rounded up or down to the nearest whole number.

Previous convictions are not usually recorded in the criminal statistics but the figures for 1978 are an exception. They give details of a sample of offenders from which it can be deduced that women are less likely than men to have a criminal record, and this is a factor affecting their sentences (Tables 2.6, 2.7).

A two per cent sample of persons convicted in 1977 of certain standard offences distinguishes first offenders from those with previous convictions. From this it can be seen that women over 21 are more likely to be first offenders than men over 21.

The proportion of first offenders (aged 21 and over) to previous offenders is 2:1 in the case of women and 1:2 in the case of men (Table 2.6). While the typical adult male offender has previous convictions, the typical adult female has none. Most male offenders begin their criminal careers in their teens, but this is not true of female offenders.

The sample of first offenders aged 21 or over convicted of shoplifting shows a similarity of sentences for men and women (Table 2.7). Of the men, 80 per cent were fined, 15 per cent were discharged and 4 per cent received

Table 2.6 Offenders convicted of non-motoring offences in 1977 by sex, age and previous convictions (Source: Home Office (1979) Table 10.2)

Offenders	Number convicted (thousands)	Estimated number of first offences		Estimated number with previous convictions	
		Thousands	% of total	Thousands	% of total
Male					
10 and under 21	188.1	85	45	103	55
21 and over	194.1	67	35	127	65
Female					
10 and under 21	24.0	17	71	7	29
21 and over	46.7	31	66	16	34

Table 2.7 Proportion of persons over 21 convicted of shoplifting in 1977, by sex, previous convictions and sentence (Source: Home Office (1979))

Sentence	Offenders			
	Without previous convictions		With previous convictions	
	Males	Females	Males	Females
Fine	80%	75%	49%	49%
Imprisonment – immediate	1%	–	17%	2%
Imprisonment – suspended	–	1%	13%	13%
Probation	4%	5%	7%	20%
Absolute or conditional discharge	15%	18%	14%	13%
Community Service Order	–	–	–	2%
Other	–	–	1%	–
Total number of persons (thousands)	12.5	19.3	15.7	8.3

probation. Of the women, 75 per cent were fined, 18 per cent were discharged and 5 per cent received probation. From this sample it appears that the disparity in disposals for men and women is markedly reduced when previous record is held constant, despite the fact that there is no control for other circumstances of the cases concerned.

For those men and women, in the sample, with previous convictions there is, however, considerable difference in the disposals (Table 2.7). Of the men, 17 per cent were given immediate imprisonment and 7 per cent were given probation. Of the women, 2 per cent were given imprisonment and 20 per cent were given probation. These differences may reflect the differences in the number and gravity of the previous convictions of the men and women concerned. However, it is impossible to ascertain this from the official statistics as they are at present produced. Nevertheless, from the difference in the distribution of sentences among male and female offenders has grown a debate on the equality of the treatment received by men and women before the courts.

The 'Chivalry' thesis

Some writers have argued that men, accustomed to giving favourable treatment to women elsewhere in society, do so in the court (Thomas, 1907; Pollak, 1950).

> One of the outstanding concomitants of the existing inequality between the sexes is chivalry and the general protective attitude of man toward woman. This attitude exists on the part of the male victim of crime as well as on the part of the officers of the law, who are still largely male in our society. Men hate to accuse women and thus indirectly send them to their punishment, police officers dislike to arrest them, district attorneys to prosecute them, judges and juries to find them guilty, and so on. (Pollak, 1950: 151)

Otto Pollak attempts to explain the pattern of female crime and punishment by reference to the position in society which he assumes that women occupy. His argument on this, as on other aspects of female criminality, is not supported by sound empirical evidence or rigorous analysis but by reference to anecdote and stereotype and a misreading of official statistics. Criticisms of this work abound (Klein, 1973; Smart, 1976; Heidensohn, 1985). However, the thesis is one which permeates speculation on the subject, and one which has been investigated by social scientists.

In a study of men and women shoplifters, Gibbens and Prince found that 21.4 per cent of the men but only 3.8 per cent of the women were sent to prison (Gibbens and Prince, 1962). Walker examined these finding in relation to the 50 per cent of the men and the 20 per cent of the women who had previous convictions and concluded that:

. . . this strongly suggests that the women were more leniently dealt with . . .

However, Farrington and Morris (1983) offer an alternative explanation of these findings. They suggest that the previously convicted men had more previous convictions, on average, than the previously convicted women; an explanation which is equally feasible given the data (Farrington and Morris, 1983:231).

One of the most widely cited pieces of research in this area is that of Stuart Nagel and Lenore Weitzman (1971). Using data from a sample of 11,258 cases from all 50 of the United States of America, Nagel and Weitzman compared the treatment received by men and women appearing before the courts on charges of assault and larceny. They found that women tended to be treated paternistically by the courts, i.e. more like children than adults. Although for both assault and larceny women were treated paternistically when compared with men – i.e. there was less likelihood of pre-trial custody, conviction, or prison if convicted – this difference was less noticeable in cases of assault than in cases of larceny. Nagel and Weitzman suggest that the harsher responses to cases of assault arise from the unwomanly nature of such crime.

Like juveniles, women were less likely to have a jury trial, and since juries are less likely to convict than the alternative, judges, this may be seen as a disadvantage of paternalism. The advantage of being treated paternistically lay in the leniency of the sentence received. White women were found to be treated more paternistically than black women, and black women more than white men. Nagel and Weitzman acknowledge that the favourable treatment received by women may be influenced by the magnitude of the offences concerned:

> ... some of the differences may have arisen from the fact that grand larcenies and felonious assaults committed by women may be generally less severe than those committed by men. Therefore, there may be generally less to merit a jury trial and less to merit a severe sentence when women are involved. (Nagel and Weitzman, 1971:180)

They also acknowledge that previous convictions may be fewer for a woman than for a man, but as information on this was not available from the data used, this factor could not be taken into consideration. However, the authors do not voice any strong misgivings about their findings which do not control for prior record and severity of offence. Nor do they suggest that future research should do so. Instead they suggest that more would be learned about the sentencing of women by analysing, not the women's offences and records, but the judges' subjectivity:

> ... perhaps future psychological questionnaire studies of judicial attitudes will throw more light on how judges subjectively view jailing and jury trials for women defendants. (Nagel and Weitzman, 1971:180)

This is in keeping with their conclusion that it is not the merits of the woman's case, but the protectiveness that she evokes in men that determine the way she is treated by the court:

> These findings seem consistent with how women are generally treated in American society. There exists a paternalistic protectiveness, at least towards white women, that assumes they need sheltering from manly experiences such as jail and from subjection to the unfriendliness of overly formal proceedings in criminal . . . cases. (Ibid.)

Despite the shortcomings of the Nagel and Weitzman study it is widely used to support the contention that women before the courts receive preferential treatment because of their sex. Rita James Simon (1977) cites this study, without any criticism of the factors considered and the conclusion reached. She then proceeds to examine the rates of conviction and types of sentences for men and women accused of the same type of offence. Her data are derived from the official statistics for California (1960–72) and Ohio (1969–71).

Simon found that women received more lenient treatment, even when they were involved in offences that might be considered more typical of men, e.g. robbery, burglary, car-theft. In this respect her results do not support the Nagel and Weitzman argument that the courts are more severe towards women who act in an un-womanly way. In other respects her findings endorse those of Nagel and Weitzman, even if she is somewhat tentative about her conclusions:

> . . . women as recently as 1972 seem to be receiving some preferential treatment at the bar of justice, and on the basis of the available data, . . . the eyes of justice are neither blinded nor fully opened; rather, they seem to be open just enough to be able to discern the sex of the defendant and to allow that characteristic to influence the decision to some extent. (Simon, 1977:67)

Like Nagel and Weitzman, Simon had not considered the effect of previous convictions, or the circumstances of the offence, and in her study the failure to consider these factors is not even mentioned.

While it is possible to challenge the 'chivalry' thesis on the inadequacy of the research which purports to demonstrate its existence, it is also possible to challenge the supposed results of such practices. Some writers have argued that it is not, as the 'chivalry' thesis proposes, to women's advantage to receive lenient treatment from the courts (Moulds, 1980; Pearson, 1976; Worrall, 1981).

Elizabeth Moulds discusses the concept of chivalry and argues that it masks an inequality in the relationships between men and women:

This focus on the benefits women presumably derive from the practice of chivalry has diverted attention from the obvious accompanying power relationship of male domination. (Moulds, 1980:280)

In an analysis of the official criminal statistics for California, Moulds attempts to compare the sentences given to men and women, controlling for race, offence and prior record. While she acknowledges that she is unable to control for the degree of crime involved in each offence, she, nevertheless, concludes that women are treated leniently. However, this leniency is deplored since it arises from a situation in which women are oppressed:

> It is true that women do enjoy certain benefits of a chivalry factor. They are arrested, prosecuted, and sent to institutions less often than are men – the benefit to them is their freedom. A major cost to them, however, is the continuation of a state of public consciousness which holds that women are less able than men and thus in need of special protective treatment. This results in extensive personal, psychological, social, economic, and political damage to the democratic notions of self-determination and equality. (Moulds, 1980:294)

It appears that even those who are critical of the supposed advantages of leniency are only too willing to accept that it occurs, despite the difficulties of controlling for those very factors which are recognised to influence sentences. Whilst some acknowledge the limitations of their research the majority find no difficulty in asserting that the sex of the woman defendant gives her an advantage when sentences are given.

Gender-role: a relevant factor

The strongest challenge to the claim that being female confers an advantage on a defendant comes from those writing on juvenile delinquents (Chesney-Lind, 1973; Smart, 1976; Shacklady-Smith, 1978; Campbell, 1981). These authors have noted the operation of a double standard by the courts whereby girls are subject to control which is related more to their gender-role than to their offences. Adolescent girls who come before the court are more likely than their male counterparts to be questioned about their sexual activity, more likely to have their offences viewed as an aspect of sexual promiscuity, and more likely to lose their liberty for activities which would not be against the law if committed by an adult. The courts appear to be concerned with enforcing a specific gender-role on those young women who engage in unfeminine behaviour since such behaviour poses a threat to their future role within the domestic sphere. My work deals with adult women appearing before the court; however, I recognise the value of recent work on younger women and girls within the criminal justice system. These studies have highlighted the way in which traditional gender roles are reinforced by police and courtroom practice. The issue of juvenile justice is beyond the scope of the present work, but it is important to recognise this as an interesting and developing field of study which has much to contribute to the debate on the social control of young women (Heidensohn, 1985; Gelsthorpe, 1984).

In a paper published in 1978, Chesney-Lind turns her attention from juvenile to adult female offenders (Chesney-Lind, 1978). In a wide-ranging review of the literature she, too, notes that many studies which claim that women receive preferential treatment fail to control for severity of offence and the number of previous convictions. In research which does control for offence and prior record, the apparent benefits to women defendants disappear (Green, 1961; Rottman and Simon, 1975; Pope, 1975 cited in Chesney-Lind, 1978). Chesney-Lind argues that it is necessary to avoid an excessively simple approach to this subject and concludes that it may be the role rather than the sex of the woman which influences the situation:

> What seems to be emerging from all of these studies is that far from treating women chivalrously the courts have been engaging in a more complex response to female criminality. It would appear that some women, particularly those who engage in traditionally female offences, may enjoy some benefits before the court, particularly if they can establish themselves as 'women' by fulfilling other traditional roles. (Chesney-Lind, 1978:216)

It is important to recognise here that the 'benefits' which may be enjoyed by women in a traditional gender-role do not necessarily give them an advantage over men, since the role imposes its own restrictions. Recognising the degree of unofficial control operating within a situation, the court may impose correspondingly less official control. This argument has been developed by Candace Kruttschnitt in her work in the USA on the sentencing of women (Kruttschnitt, 1982).

Kruttschnitt is concerned with the inter-relationship between economic dependency, frequently found in women, and informal and formal social control.

> Sex is, of course, a biological characteristics, but it is also associated with social characteristics. Economic dependency is one such gender-related characteristic which, at the same time, connotes informal social control . . . The quantity of informal social control inherent in a dependency status may explain the sentences that female criminal defendants incur. (Kruttschnitt, 1982:497)

Kruttschnitt argues that it is not the amount but the source of a woman's income which affects the degree of informal control within her life, i.e. whether she is seen to be supported by another, since such support is understood to involve control. In an analysis of probation officers' reports, Kruttschnitt found that less formal (i.e. state-imposed) control was recommended for those women in a situation of strong economic dependency. The results of this work lead Kruttschnitt to conclude that the sentences received by women are a recognition of their role rather than their sex:

> ... The findings ... suggest ... that the legal system prefers to exert little social control over women whose lives presently contain an indicator of daily social control such as that entailed by economic dependency. (Kruttschnitt, 1982:510)

By recognising the significance of the woman's gender-role we may achieve a better understanding of a factor which has recently been revealed as relevant in the sentencing of women, i.e. the marital status of the defendant.

In a recent study Ilene Nagel examined the judicial processing of 2,965 defendants (2,627 men and 338 women) in a major city in New York State (Nagel, 1981). The analysis included variables related to the social attributes of the defendants, e.g. marital status, family composition, age, race and employment status, as well as variables related to the criminal career, e.g. type of offence, previous record and other cases pending. Having attempted to control for these variables Nagel found that women were likely to receive lighter sentences than men and that prior convictions had a more negative effect on the sentencing of men than of women. However, she acknowledges that this result may have been influenced by the methods used:

> ... the fact that prior convictions was so much stronger for males than for females may be a function of males having prior convictions for *more offences* and for *more serious offences*. By coding the variable as we did, variation in the number of prior convictions and the severity of the offence for which the defendant was convicted (felony versus misdemeanour) was obscured. Since we know that males have more prior convictions and more convictions for felonies, it may be that the effect was stronger because the record was more severe. (Nagel, 1981:112, Original emphasis.)

The analysis also found that being married had more advantage for a woman being sentenced than for a man:

... marital status had no significant effect for males and a strong and significant effect for females – married females were considerably less likely than their unmarried female counterparts to spend any time imprisoned ... (Ibid:113)

The advantage here is not of the woman over the man, but of the married woman over the single woman.

David Farrington and Allison Morris came to a similar conclusion concerning the influence of marital status (Farrington and Morris, 1983). Like Nagel, who also undertook research on differential sentencing, their discovery of the effect of marital status was a by-product of the study.

Using court records Farrington and Morris examined the cases of 395 different persons, including 108 women, who had been sentenced for offences of theft in Cambridge City Magistrates' Court between January and July 1979. The aim of the research was to discover whether the sex of the defendant influenced the severity of the sentence and the likelihood of re-conviction. Unlike many who work in this area, Farrington and Morris recognised the importance and difficulty of adequately controlling for offence and previous conviction:

> ... the primary aim of this research was to investigate whether the sex of the defendant was related to sentencing ... independently of other variables. It was therefore necessary to carry out a multivariate analysis with categorical variables, which is not straightforward. Parametric techniques ... have underlying statistical assumptions, such as that variables are measured on interval scales and are normally distributed, which are clearly violated by categorical data. (Farrington and Morris, 1983:234)

Recognising the limitations of each of a number of techniques, Farrington and Morris decided to combine the strengths of different methods:

> ... the analysis used dichotomous dependent variables, least squares multiple regression for large-scale multivariate analysis, and logistic regression to check the key results in smaller scale analyses. Finally, loglinear modelling was used to assess whether the results were affected by having a dependent variable with more than two categories. (Ibid:235)

They found that while 36.9 per cent of the men received severe sentences, only 15.7 per cent of the women were sentenced severely; however, this was not a demonstration of leniency towards the women, but the consequence of the men's criminal histories:

> ... the sex of the defendant did not have any direct influence on the severity of the sentence or the probability of reconviction. Women only appear to

receive more lenient sentences and to have a lower likelihood of reconviction because they had committed less serious offences and were less likely to have been convicted previously. (Ibid:245)

Unlike Nagel, Farrington and Morris found that previous convictions and other factors were important in the sentencing of both men and women, but like Nagel they found that domestic circumstances were more important in the sentencing of women than men:

> While some factors (notably previous convictions) had an important influence on sentence severity and re-conviction for both men and women, others only had an influence for one sex. In particular, marital status, family background and children were more important for women than for men. (Ibid:246)

Farrington and Morris offer a tentative explanation for the severe sentences given to women whose backgrounds did not conform to the expected familial role:

> Women who were in the 'other' category on marital status (predominantly divorced or separated rather than widowed) received relatively severe sentences, as did women from a deviant family background (coming from a broken home, usually). *It could be that the magistrates disapproved of these categories of women offenders.* (Ibid:245, Emphasis added.)

However, I would suggest that the magistrates are doing more than expressing disapproval in their sentencing. Like Kruttschnitt (1982), discussed above, I think it probable that the degree of formal control is a recognition of the informal control imposed by the more acceptable roles. This was illustrated by the following case which occurred during my fieldwork.

A man and two women appeared before the magistrates charged with shoplifting; the case was to be tried at the Crown Court. The police asked that bail be refused to the man, Mr Green, and to one of the women, Mrs Day, since both defendants had a long history of previous offences, and of offending while on bail. They asked that the second woman, Miss Boyle, be given bail on condition that she report daily to her local police station. Mr Day was in court, and he was invited to speak. He asked the court to grant bail to his wife because he and their four children needed her at home. The magistrate commented, 'Children place a different complexion on it'. At the end of that first court appearance Mr Green was refused bail (he had no fixed address and no family commitments) and the two women, who each had four children, were given bail on specific conditions. Mrs Day was to report twice a day to her local police station, and Miss Boyle was to report once a day to her local police station.

It was their second appearance in court that the magistrates' attitude to family life and social control was fully revealed. A week after their first appearance both women applied to have their reporting restrictions lifted. Each woman argued that caring for four children was very difficult if she had to go to the police station each day. Mrs Day had her reporting restrictions lifted as her husband was prepared to stand surety for £500. Miss Boyle was refused any alteration in her bail conditions. So, at the end of their second appearance Mrs Day, who had originally been regarded as the more culpable by the police, who had opposed her bail application, was subject to less official control than Miss Boyle, who still had to report daily. Both women were involved in childcare, but Mrs Day was living in a conventional family unit, while Miss Boyle, a single parent, was not. In their attitude to the defendants in this case, and particularly in their different responses to the two women, the magistrates demonstrated their assumptions about the degree of unofficial control to which family members, and especially women, are subject.

In the chapters that follow I will argue that family circumstances are important in presenting both men and women to the court, but within the family, men and women are ascribed very different roles. The consequence for a woman, of playing her traditional gender role within the family, is a degree of unofficial but effective control which the courts seem to recognise when passing sentence. While some may argue that such control is a good thing for those found guilty of criminal offences, we are still left with the problem of such control in the lives of women who never come before the court. The oppression of women within the family has a significance beyond debates on sentencing, judicial process and criminal justice systems.

Conclusion

The official statistics on crime reveal something of the differences in the patterns of conviction and sentence for men and women. These differences make it difficult to compare the sentences of men and women since these defendants differ not only in the sentences they receive but also in the type and severity of offences with which they are charged, and in their criminal record. From the work considered here, it appears that the claims that women offenders receive preferential treatment because of their sex are unfounded. When the relevant influences on sentencing are adequately considered the differences on grounds of sex are removed (Chesney-Lind, 1978; Farrington and Morris, 1983). However, the influence of marital status and domestic circumstances is an interesting factor which has emerged in recent research. By recognising this factor, the court is acknowledging the degree of control exerted upon a woman within her traditional role.

Analysing sentencing differentials is a traditional but limited way of addressing the issue of the equality of men and women defendants. Much of the work is limited by a failure to control effectively for the relevant factors. However, even those studies which are rigorous in their methodology are unable to explain the findings, relating to marital status, which they discover. The limitation arises because of the focus on the sentence, i.e. the end product of the judicial process. To appreciate fully the significance of this process it is necessary to give attention to the interactions by which it is constructed. In the next chapter the focus is on the process of summary justice, i.e. on magistrates' courts.

Chapter Three

The magistrates' court

The magistrates' courts in this country deal with over 90 per cent of criminal cases. All defendants appear before magistrates and those charged with summary offences must have their cases heard there. Those charged with very serious offences will be committed to the crown court for a trial; in such cases (like the one described in Chapter 2) the magistrates will decide whether the defendants should be granted bail or remanded in custody until the trial. Other defendants, charged with triable-either-way offences, may choose between having their case heard by the magistrates or going to a crown court to appear before a judge and jury. Many are persuaded to choose the magistrates' court because they intend to plead guilty, or because the case will be heard sooner, or because they believe that they will get a lighter sentence. The result is that most criminal cases in England and Wales are heard and sentenced by a group of men and women with little training in law and no accountability to the local community for which they sit as representatives.

The majority of magistrates are lay justices of the peace, selected from among those who apply to sit on the local bench. In most cases the membership of the selection committee and the criteria by which it operates, are kept secret. Although there is an expressed aim, by the Lord Chancellor's Office, that the constituency of the bench should reflect the

Table 3.1 Distribution of cases (excluding summary motoring) between Crown Courts and Magistrates' Courts (Source: Home Office, 1985: Tables 6.1 and 6.b.)

	Court			
Year	Crown Courts		Magistrates' Courts	
	Number (in thousands)	Percentage	Number (in thousands)	Percentage
1974	56.4	6%	824	94%
1975	63.1	7%	878	93%
1976	68.0	7%	925	93%
1977	68.7	7%	940	93%
1978	69.1	7%	908	93%
1979	62.9	7%	901	93%
1980	73.9	7%	1,009	93%
1981	78.9	7%	995	93%
1982	82.8	8%	1,008	92%
1983	88.8	8%	1,051	92%
1984	90.5	8%	1,004	92%

local community, magistrates are still drawn mainly from the white middle-class (Baldwin, 1976; Bartlett and Walker, 1973; Burney, 1979; King and May, 1985).

Other regular participants in the magistrates' courts include:

the clerk to the court who sits in front of the magistrates and who advises them on matters of law and procedure;

the warrant officer who ensures that all participants are ready and who arranges the order in which cases are heard;

the ushers who bring defendants and witnesses into the court at the appropriate point in proceedings;

the police officers present to give evidence;

the probation officer present to submit a social inquiry report that was requested at a previous sitting, or who may be required to give assistance should the magistrates require it;

lawyers to speak for those who can afford to pay them, or those who have been granted legal aid;

a journalist from a local paper who may be present for all or part of the proceedings;

and, of course, the defendants.

It is the magistrates who decide on the guilt or innocence of a defendant in a contested case, and it is they who decide on the appropriate sentence in all cases. Such decisions may be influenced by a number of factors and lawyers and probation officers may be given the opportunity of presenting information and arguments which they consider relevant. Ultimately, however, the responsibility for sentence lies with the magistrates.

The positions occupied by members of the court, and their autonomy within the court, can be seen as a reflection of the relative positions held by those individuals outside the court. Lawyers, probation officers and the police belong to groups with different statuses and loyalties. The magistrates and the defendants appear as lay men and women, but in most instances the differences in their status and power within the court correspond to differences in status and power outside the court. Magistrates, the majority of whom are middle class, sit in judgement on defendants, the majority of whom are working class. There are more men than women magistrates, nevertheless women account for a higher proportion of magistrates than of any other legal or judicial position. In 1977 the proportion of women to men was 1:1.7 (Skryme, 1979:47). Since most defendants are men, the authority of these women might be seen as a contravention of their gender-role. However, gender divisions are mediated by class divisions and while it is unusual for even middle-class women to hold the degree of power associated with the magistracy, the exercise of this power is, in most cases, in relation to working-class men. Inter-class relationships are thus reinforced. This becomes clearer when magistrates discuss their different reactions to middle-class and working-class defendants (see Chapter 6).

Reproducing social divisions

Magistrates' courts are part of the apparatus of state control. It is in these courts that the formal rules of society – the laws – are endorsed; it is here, too, that the informal, unwritten rules regulating social relations are re-enacted. This becomes apparent when the focus changes from a concern with the end results of the criminal justice system – the sentences – to an interest in the process by which court business is conducted. In her study of the interactions within magistrates' courts, Pat Carlen (1976) describes how mundane procedures function as a means of social control. The spatial arrangements of the court-room, and the routines of judicial procedure reinforce the power differentials between the different groups:

> In hierarchically organised social institutions . . . certain people can mono-
> polise and manipulate the scenic and scheduling arrangements of the most

important public settings, so that a coercive control, often spurious to the professed aims of the institution, can be maintained. (Carlen, 1976:19)

While the rhetoric of the court is that the defendant will receive a fair trial, will be given the opportunity to oppose the prosecution, and is innocent until proved guilty; the reality of the situation is that a hostile environment, and ignorance of the routine procedure recognised by the court, combine to render the defendant helpless in the situation.

> In magistrates' courts, where the vast majority of defendants do not have a solicitor as a 'mouthpiece', defendants are set up in a guarded dock and then, at a distance artificially stretched beyond the boundaries of face-to-face communication, asked to describe or comment on intimate details of their lives; details which do not in themselves constitute infraction of any law but which are open to public investigation once a person has been *accused* of breaking the law. (Ibid:23, Original emphasis.)

Power resides with those whose authority is derived from the court or recognised by the court. These are the actors who make effective use of the court procedure to accomplish their ends: ends which, since they may be accomplished by this procedure, do not pose any threat or alternative to the social reality that the court endorses. While the rhetoric of the court is that the legal process ensures that all receive a fair hearing, the reality of its procedures is that competing definitions of social reality are unheard. Carlen uses the concept of the 'restricted code' (Bernstein, 1971) to discuss the function of this particular mode of linguistic communication.

> The formal language of the law creates the boundaries of formal symbolic control in the courts. The written, codified procedural rules for the administration of justice allow for the imposition of a *restricted* linguistic code whose lexicon and organising structure are wholly predictable. (Carlen, 1976:102, Original emphasis.)

However, this code is not imposed on all members of the court at all times. Instead it is imposed if there is a challenge to the smooth functioning of the court. Such challenges usually come from the defendant. Carlen quotes Mary Douglas (1970) in support of the contention that the imposition of the restricted code inhibits challenge to the consensus.

> The restricted code is deeply enmeshed in the immediate social structure; utterances have a double purpose: they convey information, yes, but they also express the social structure, embellish and re-inforce it ... the second function is the dominant one. (Douglas, 1970, quoted in Carlen, 1976:129)

Thus, the use of language in the process of justice serves to reinforce and reproduce the status quo. Social control is camouflaged by practices which covertly perpetuate power differentials:

> (The court) is an institutional setting charged with the maintenance and reproduction of existing forms of structural dominance . . . Transformation of the ritual display of justice into the socio-legal technology of coercion is the first step in the manufacture and celebration of all magistrates' justice. (Carlen, 1976:38)

In a study of the law at work in the courts, Doreen McBarnet supports Carlen's description of the use of rules in magistrates' courts, but goes on to examine the rules that are in use (McBarnet, 1981). She questions a situation in which the state insists on a formal legal procedure, and pays for the provision of magistrates, clerk and police prosecution, but demurs at providing automatic legal aid.

> If the defendant, normally unrepresented, is the only one who does not know the rules, as every study of courts demonstrates, the cause must be traced beyond his ignorance, or the court team's games, to the paradox of a legal structure which requires knowledge of procedural propriety in making a case, and a legal policy which denies access to it. (McBarnet, 1981:124)

McBarnet discusses the role that is played by the high courts. In a democratic society, the higher courts become the site for the demonstration of the principles of equality and justice from which the state derives its authority.

> One of the essential justifications of the democratic state is precisely that it is based on legality, that the relationship between the state and the individuals of civil society is one governed not by the arbitrary exercise of power but by power exercised within the constraints of the law. (Ibid:8)

However, McBarnet finds that the practice of law does not exemplify the legal rhetoric which claims to guard the civil liberties of each citizen.

> By examining the law not just in terms of the general principles of its own ideology, but in terms of the details of its specific structures, procedures, and decisions this analysis has tried to show that the law governing the production, preparation and presentation of evidence does not live up to its own rhetoric. (Ibid:154)

While many people are familiar with the rhetoric of justice (e.g. that someone is innocent until proven guilty, that all are equal before the law) very few are familiar with legal practice which allows re-definitions and exceptions to subvert such general principles so that the accused's silence is a factor in proving guilt and previous convictions become grounds for defining behaviour as an offence. And if the legal process fails to live up to its own rhetoric in the crown courts, with the full panoply of judicial ritual, what is the situation in the magistrates' courts in which the majority of defendants have their cases heard?

Magistrates' courts are concerned with summary justice, with the routine and trivial business of the community. Because of the supposedly trivial nature of their work, the principles of legality, applied in the crown courts, are not deemed necessary. One of these principles is the representation of the defendant by a legally competent advocate to ensure a fair trial. However, many of the defendants in the magistrates' courts are confused or fatalistic about the role they could play in their own defence, and many plead guilty just to get matters over quickly (Dell, 1971). Because of the importance attributed to the proceedings in the higher courts, despite the small proportion of cases dealt with there, the greater injustices and anomalies of the lower courts go unheeded:

> Legal policy has established two tiers of justice. One, the higher courts, is for public consumption, the arena where the ideology of justice is put on display. The other, the lower courts, deliberately structured in defiance of the ideology of justice, is concerned less with subtle ideological messages than with direct control. (McBarnet, 1981:153)

In a footnote McBarnet modifies her claim tht the lower courts are not concerned with ideological messages. She adds that these messages are not, as they are in the high court, related to law and justice but:

> They *do* fill other ideological roles, e.g. on the virtues of employment and family life. (McBarnet, 1981:171, Original emphasis.)

I agree that the lower courts, the magistrates' courts, are concerned with control, and I will argue that much of this control involves a particular model of family life – a model which is constantly reinforced by the daily practice of the court; a model which defines women as primarily domestic and subordinate to men.

By appreciating the role played by the routines of summary justice in the social control and reproduction of society, it is possible to have a better understanding of the treatment received by women defendants in a magistrates' court.

Both Carlen (1976) and McBarnet (1981) have demonstrated how different features of the routines of summary justice operate to reinforce social divisions. The contradictions between legal rhetoric and legal reality result in a systematic disadvantaging of the powerless. I will argue that magistrates' courts are involved not only in the reproduction of class divisions, but also in the reproduction of gender divisions.

At Hillbury Court

My work is based on a case study of a magistrates' court situated in a town on the edge of the Greater London conurbation. (A fuller description is given in the Research Appendix.)

The period of observation consisted of one or two mornings a week during 1980 and 1981. During that time I saw a total of 321 complete cases: these involved 210 men and 111[1] women defendants. Eight men and eight women appeared as co-defendants. Three of these couples were legally represented, and 32 of the other men and 25 of the other women were legally represented. Social inquiry reports were requested for 37 of the men and 35 of the women.

It was unusual to find cases in which the defendants resembled each other in all respects but sex. Most of the men had previous convictions and most of the women were appearing for the first time. This reflected the national pattern noted in Chapter 2. From the 80 cases of shoplifting seen during the period of observation, 54 per cent of the men but only 16 per cent of the women had more than two previous offences, while only 25 per cent of the men, but 59 per cent of the women, were being charged with their first offence.

Family circumstances and disposable income were rarely similar for men and women and this affected the sentences. Fines are the most usual penalty given by the court, but many magistrates commented in interview on the difficulty of fining a woman with no disposable income. The women before them were usually responsible for the care and maintenance of children, supported either by social security benefits or by such small housekeeping allowances that to deduct any amount to pay a fine would be to deprive the children.

Magistrates frequently said that they responded to the circumstances of the case and not the sex of the offender and my observations confirmed this. On the few occasions on which men and women appeared in similar circumstances, they received similar sentences. This applied to defendants appearing on separate charges and to those appearing as co-defendants on joint charges. In cases involving a co-defendant of the opposite sex the blame for originating and executing the offence was not automatically ascribed to either the man or the woman. The magistrates appeared to accept that either could be the dominant partner, and that in most cases each was equally culpable.[2]

The majority of cases, involving men and women, were treated in a routine manner, with little discussion of individual circumstances. Defendants of either sex who appeared on charges involving drunkenness appeared as the first business of each day. They usually pleaded guilty, were unrepresented, and were despatched with a fine of £10 for being drunk and £15–£40 for being drunk and disorderly (depending on the extent of the alleged disorderliness). Minor drug offences were also the subject of routine treatment. Most men and women were fined £25 or £30 for a first offence of possessing cannabis.

Less routine matters give rise to discussion among the participants in the social construction of justice, and in so doing reveal something of the criteria by which decisions are reached. However, even in such matters it was usually the personal, or rather the family circumstances, rather than the sex of the defendant, which were considered, together with the offence and previous record, in deciding a sentence.

Magistrates were concerned with the economic situation and domestic responsibilities of defendants, and these were discussed by lawyers in court or presented in social inquiry reports by probation officers. In interview many magistrates said that they would be influenced by the presence of children if the defendant was responsible for child-care. The cases observed showed this was apparent whether the defendant was male or female. The circumstances that alert magistrates to the need for a social inquiry report are circumstances which suggest the presence of social problems, typically financial and emotional stress in a situation involving child-care. Such circumstances are more frequently found in cases involving female defendants. In such cases differential treatment arises out of the different circumstances, which are related to the different roles of men and women.

However, the evidence of similar treatment for the few men and women who appear before the court in similar circumstances may satisfy the court's criteria of justice but it has little to do with the way in which the subordinate role of women is reproduced by the processes of summary justice. The reproduction of gender differences is a subtle process accomplished not by overt sentencing disparities, but by the routine processes of the court. To understand this it is necessary to go beyond those rare cases in which men and women appear in similar circumstances and consider the ways in which most men and women are presented to the court. It is necessary to become alert to the ideology which underlies the perceptions and interpretations of court personnel and which is manifest in the language of those whose words play an important part in the judicial process.

My concern is not so much with the minority of cases in which men and women appear in similar circumstances, but with the way in which the majority of cases are processed, and with the social relations which are endorsed by such practice. These are revealed by the routines of the court – in pronouncements from the bench, in pleas of mitigation, in the arguments contained in social inquiry reports – all of which, by their congruence and compatibility, reaffirm the coherence of the apparent consensus. Of course, individual magistrates, lawyers or probation officers may privately dissent from the prevailing world-view. However, all are well aware of what is acceptable to the court and it is this shared model which informs, and is revealed by, their utterances. In the following chapters this model will be discussed as it is discovered in the arguments, attitudes and assumptions of lawyers, probation officers and magistrates.

Chapter Four

Pleas of mitigation[1]

The language of the courtroom both reflects and reinforces the prevailing picture of the social order. It contains and communicates the attitudes and assumptions of those involved in the social construction of justice. Pleas of mitigation play a useful role in displaying the rhetoric of the court and thereby revealing the ideological structuring of the judicial process. Such pleas are made in open court, in the hope of influencing the decision of the magistrates. The material presented is that which is deemed appropriate to the occasion by the lawyer, and this may be accepted or rejected by the magistrates. In some cases the magistrates will rebuke the lawyer or refute an argument as ill-founded or inappropriate, but in most cases the magistrates will indicate that they accept the logic of the plea. This may be done explicitly by direct comment or implicitly by allowing the lighter sentence for which the plea was made. Such pleas, and the responses to them, form part of a public discourse in the social construction of justice in our society. By these pleas the offence and the offender are placed in a context which is then offered as an explanation of the crime and/or an indication of an appropriate sentence. Implicit in these pleas is a model of the social world, and particularly of the family, in which behaviour is measured by a commonly held value system, and in which each defendant has an appropriate role to play.

Pleas of mitigation invoke a consensual social world in which the family is the basic unit, a privileged unit and the touchstone of normality. Mitigating circumstances reflect the defendant's relationship to the social world. Should this relationship follow an acceptable pattern it will be used to show that the defendant is not really a criminal since the social identity in question is basically conformist. Criminal activity will be presented as a temporary aberration. A conventional life-style is presented as evidence of adequate socialisation. The absence of such socialisation may be inferred from a life-style at variance with the model of normality implicit in pleas of mitigation. The abnormality of the defendant's relationship may then be used to deny full criminal responsibility.

Mitigating circumstances at Hillbury

In the cases observed 63 defendants were legally represented. In all but seven cases the pleas of mitigation were based on the family circumstances of the defendants. The seven exceptions concerned 4 men and 3 women, appearing separately, for whom such pleas would have been inappropriate. In three cases the pleas were for a disposition that provided treatment rather than punishment, these concerned two registered drug addicts and an alcoholic. In two cases the offence was presented as a response to debt. In another case the defendant was described as someone who had readily admitted his guilt and shown his penitence by making full restitution of the money stolen. In one case the lawyer voiced his recognition of the

Table 4.1 Distribution of arguments used in pleas of mitigation

Argument used in plea	Sex of Defendant	
	Male	Female
Family circumstances	31	25
Physical illness	–	5
Mental illness	2	3
Alcoholism	2	1
Drug addiction	1	1
Debt	1	1
Restitution made	1	–
No mitigation possible	1	–
TOTAL	35	28

Hillbury magistrates court

difficulty of making any plea on behalf of someone with no family ties and no job; he simply asked that the defendant be given a second chance.

For the majority of defendants the pleas of mitigation were based on their family circumstances. Such pleas used a number of different arguments in relation to the family, and to other circumstances, such as the physical or mental health of the defendant. The tables give an indication of the relative frequency with which different arguments were used in this context.

Table 4.2 Distribution of arguments relating to the family, used in pleas of mitigation

Arguments used in pleas	Sex of defendant	
	Male	Female
Family Circumstances		
I The family as the site of social responsibility	12	16
II The family as the site of social control	15	9
III Working for the family	8	8
IV The family as a privileged institution	3	–
V The family as an enduring unit	8	8
VI The basic family unit as a man and a woman	13	12
Other	4	3
TOTAL	35	28

Already it is apparent that the arguments addressed in mitigation by lawyers are similar for both men and women. Before considering the implications of this further, the substance of the six types of argument used about family circumstances will be considered.

I The family as the site of social responsibility

Family circumstances formed the focus of most pleas for men and women and frequently constituted the mitigation. A lawyer would emphasise the part played by the defendant in the family life. The recognition of responsibilities and duties would be stressed to assure the court that the defendant was really a normal member of society and the current case was out of character. Typically the defendant would be shown to be playing an appropriate role in relation to the other family members. This might be that of spouse, parent, or child. In the following case the lawyer described the filial duty shown by her clients in order to emphasise their non-criminal identity. She then argued that a forthcoming marriage should be seen as a guarantee against occasional criminal behaviour. It would serve, she argued, as an effective social control.

Tony Woods (aged 25) and Rob Woods (aged 30), brothers, had pleaded guilty to charges of actual bodily harm and malicious wounding. Since they each had a number of previous convictions their counsel endeavoured to show that the incident which had resulted in the charges was out of character in their present reformed lives. Addressing the bench she said:

> [The defendants' father] is an invalid – he came to the assistance of someone being raped and was injured by the rapist. He received £4,000 compensation. The mother recently had TB and the boys supported both parents until she was fit enough to get a job . . . They are a close-knit family, good to each other . . . As the bench realises the drink usually causes the trouble.

The barrister told the court that Tony was engaged to be married to a young woman who was a good influence:

> Eileen will not tolerate 'trouble'. She made Tony give himself up, and his brother came with him. She would not stand for trouble.

The defendants' mother was then called to the stand where she emphasised the familial duty shown by her sons. She told the court how her sons had supported their parents financially, and continued:

> Tony put off his marriage until we were alright, although I begged him not to because he wants to have children . . . They are quiet in the house, far from violent.

When sentencing the magistrate said that the defendants' appearances were becoming frequent and similar, and that it had been difficult to decide between a fine and a short term of imprisonment. However, each defendant was fined £200 with a warning that this was their last chance.

II The family as the site of social control

The idea that a spouse will act as a guardian in preventing re-offending was suggested in cases involving both men and women. In the next case it is one of several factors introduced. Other factors mentioned included those most frequently found in pleas of mitigation: the defendant is seen as trustworthy and responsible by an employer; the defendant has suffered from an unhappy family in the past; the defendant meets her family obligations. In this case there was also a reference to the defendant's medical condition. However, it is the promise of care and control in marriage that elicits the magistrates' response. Initially they seem to favour such informal, but effective, control over the formal control of a probation order.

Susan Smith (aged 30) had pleaded guilty to the theft of two vases valued at £19. She had several previous convictions and had served prison sentences for burglary, forgery and theft. It was three and a half years since she was released from prison. A social inquiry report and a medical report had been prepared. Her lawyer addressed the court:

. . . In this instance she was not behaving furtively but openly taking things. There are medical reports and a letter from her employer . . . My client came to Hillbury to meet someone to shop for a wedding dress. She has mental difficulties and found herself in the store with items that she didn't want. She came to her senses but could not face returning the items. She was in no way furtive and the medical report refers to her compulsion to steal. She has a bad record but the difference between these and previous crimes is the matter of personal gain. She did not want these items and the theft is from compulsion.

Her background is pathetic. She lost her four week old son and her husband blamed her and beat her for six months before leaving her. Two years ago her mother died of cancer leaving an elderly father alone. He is dependent upon her and one reason for not sending her to prison is that she visits him daily and is always available by phone . . . Her present employers think highly of her and allow her to handle up to £800 over a week. They know about her past.

Yet she steals £19 worth of goods she did not want. The medical report indicates that this is a pyschiatric disturbance that should be amenable to treatment. She has worked hard to make good in difficult circumstances since she came out of prison. She is engaged to be married to someone who doesn't want her to get into trouble. He is extremely supportive. He accompanies her on her weekly shop. If she went to prison she would lose her home and her job. She needs psychiatric help.

The magistrates replied that they felt they had two options. They could either adopt the recommendation of the social inquiry report and give a probation order with psychiatric treatment, or, as they were impressed with the description of the defendant's fiancé, they could defer sentence:

> as she is getting married to someone who will look after her.

The magistrates said that they favoured the latter course. The lawyer urged the probation order and this was, a little reluctantly, given.

As in the preceding case, where magistrates believe that the defendants are likely to reform there is the possibility of sentence being deferred until a later date. This deferment of sentence was often used in cases in which the defendants seemed likely to demonstrate their reform by becoming members of an approved family unit. In the following examples the defence lawyer emphasised the new found conventionality of his clients, in contrast to their former unorthodox life-styles associated with criminality.

When Phil Lane (18) and Mandy Street (17) first came before Hillbury Court they faced charges of theft of men's clothing from a chain store. Both had previous convictions, and Mandy Street had run away from home. At the time of their first appearance in court Mandy was pregnant, and the defendants were presented to the court as a couple about to marry and 'settle down'. Sentence was deferred for six months to see if there would be a change in their life-style. It was this change that their lawyer attempted to convey to the court when they reappeared for sentence, six months later:

> They are now a responsible couple, living in accommodation for the homeless, but soon to be moving to a council flat in East London. [Phil] has applied and been accepted for a government re-training scheme which will qualify him as a bricklayer. [Mandy] is a full-time mother. The child has demanded a response and resurrected responsibilities in the couple. They are now a team rather than two drifting individuals thrown together by circumstances.

At this point the magistrate interrupted:

> What about their intention to get married?

The lawyer replied:

> They are working in reverse order from most people and this will happen when the flat has been settled.

The magistrate persisted:

> My question concerned the stability that marriage creates.

However, the magistrates were satisfied that a new and acceptable life-
style was being adopted, and a probation order was made to give further
assistance.

III Working for the family

Most pleas of mitigation discuss the defendant's employment record.
Evidence of continued employment and the trust of employers will be put
forward whenever possible. However, these virtues of diligence and trustworthiness are shown in relation to the family. For men and women paid
employment was recognised as a means of providing for the family in an
appropriately responsible manner, a further indication of a non-criminal
identity.

Peter Day (aged 30) pleaded guilty to several charges arising out of an
incident when he failed to stop for a policeman when driving dangerously
in the wrong direction down a one-way street. The policeman was slightly
injured. The defence laywer called the defendant's employer as a character
witness. The employer referred to Peter as 'an exemplary employee' who
was 'hard-working and trustworthy'. Three other, written, testimonials
were produced. The lawyer argued that this act was not typical of his
client's behaviour:

> This was out of character as he works very hard and is a family man. He is
> ashamed, concerned and contrite . . .

The bench retired to decide on a sentence and on their return they told the
court:

> We've given careful consideration to all the facts, and in view of the
> defendant's personal life and record we will deal leniently with this matter.

A fine of £215 was imposed, and an order that £100 compensation be paid to
the policeman. The defendant did not lose his licence since this would have
made it difficult for him to get to work. By demonstrating his acceptable
familial role the defendant was able to avoid the full consequences of his
criminal actions.

IV The family as a privileged institution

While many aspects of family life are covered by law there are areas where
the state seems reluctant to interfere with the internal constraints and

patterns of family life. A spouse can not be compelled to testify against the other partner (Cross, 1979:173). Rape within marriage is not a recognised crime.[2] Lawyers would seek to reduce the gravity of an offence by pointing out that it occurred within the context of a family dispute. The loyalties and values engendered within the family, which make it an effective agent of social control are also recognised as providing an excuse for behaviour that might otherwise be reprehensible. In the next example the defendant's behaviour is so excused, although non-family members were involved.

Denis Cook (aged 48) pleaded guilty to assaulting his son's tenant, and the policeman who had been called when tempers flared. The lawyer stressed the 'family nature' of the dispute in mitigation of the violence that had occurred:

> . . . This was a domestic dispute with involvement of a father in his son's business. My client lived on the top floor, the victim on the middle floor and the son on the ground floor. The son suspected the tenant of fiddling the meter since the yield had fallen from £3.50 per week, to 50p per week. My client grew angry because (the tenant) called the police, he lost his temper when (the tenant) seemed to be smiling . . .

The defendant was described as a man in steady employment as a park-keeper, and character witnesses were called. The first was his superior at work who testified to the diligence and trustworthiness of the defendant. A local JP also testified that the action in question was 'out-of-character' in a man whom he knew to be kind, courteous, and well-respected.

On passing sentence the magistrates said:

> We feel that there are mitigating circumstances and so we will just fine you £50 for each offence . . .

Behaviour which would have been reprehensible outside the context of the family is viewed differently when 'family feelings' are involved.

V The family as an enduring unit

Despite the increasing incidence of marital breakdown the family invoked in pleas of mitigation is a unit characterised by resilience. Even when the offence has violated the norms of family life there is still the hope that all may be well, and that this will be achieved by the maintenance or re-establishment of a normal family life. The basic unit of this family is the man and the woman.

Dave Jones (aged 37) pleaded guilty to two cases of indecent assault on his 13-year-old daughter. These incidents were blamed on the alcohol that he drank in order to relax after working hard. The offence led to his leaving the family home and he was described, on his first appearance in court, as a man whose life was in ruins, since he had lost his wife and his daughter. His defence counsel stressed that Dave was not a 'typical criminal' and had a previous good character.

> He has no previous convictions. These actions are the result of drinking, and the drinking is the result of hard work and pressure. He's working a 16-hour shift and needs to drink in order to relax. He suffers pressure from living with his father-in-law . . .

The case was remanded for a social inquiry report. On Dave Jones's second appearance the court was told, by his lawyer, that the daughter was living with her grandmother, and the husband and wife were attempting to re-establish the marriage. This met with explicit approval from the bench:

> It's probably a good thing that you're trying to patch up your marriage.

There was no reference to the separation of mother and daughter. A probation order, for three years, was made.

In this case the magistrates' faith in the durability of marriage was particularly blind. I saw a copy of the social inquiry report which they had before them. In this the wife was described as adamant about pursuing divorce proceedings; she had told the probation officer that her husband was being given temporary shelter under her roof, and that they were sleeping in separate rooms. Despite the written evidence to the contrary the lawyer argued that a reconciliation had taken place. It was to this argument that the magistrates responded.

VI   *The basic family unit is a man and a woman*

This assumption was apparent in the previous example and can be recognised in the cases discussed below. It is also present in situations where alternative models of family are found wanting, not because of lack of care but because of a lack of conformity. Lesbian mothers, for example, find it difficult to obtain custody because they are considered unable to provide socialisation into 'normal family life' (Brophy and Smart, 1981; Brophy, 1986). The same attitude is apparent in Helen Dunne's case discussed below.

Those deprived of the support of a conventional family unit, i.e. a man and a woman, especially if they are involved in the rearing of children, are recognised as vulnerable to distress and temptation. Such deprivation may have occurred in childhood or it may be a feature of the defendant's adult life.

In the next example the defendant's attempts to play her role as a good home-maker are emphasised but she is shown to be handicapped by the lack of financial and emotional support of a man.

Belle Waters (aged 33) pleaded guilty to the theft of linen and children's clothes from a chain store. Her lawyer told the court that the defendant's life had been a series of domestic crises:

> She is receiving treatment for depression and in 1973 she attempted suicide by an overdose of drugs. Her first marriage, in 1964, lasted six years and ended in divorce because of mental and physical cruelty which was so bad that the court ordered that her husband should not see the children, and he has provided no maintenance . . . With (her present husband) life is catastrophic. He works infrequently. He pays no bills although he could earn good money as a builder. They have received threats of services being cut off. . . He disappears leaving her to cope when things get bad. She is forced to work in a pub at lunch-time for £30 a week. This and family allowance is all she has to support herself and her children. She feels the children are deprived . . . The things she took were 'on impulse', the act was not premeditated . . .

The magistrates requested a social inquiry report, and when Belle Waters next came to court she was given a probation order in recognition of the help she needed. However, this help was proffered because of her role within the family rather than her identity as female. Pleas based on 'the frailty of woman' without the concurrent domestic responsibilities were not sympathetically received by the magistrates. The defendants in the next two examples were both attractive young women who stood tearfully and apologetically in the dock.

When first arrested for shoplifting Michelle Knight (aged 20) had denied stealing two blouses, valued at £78. The court heard that she had advanced a number of stories to account for their presence in her car and had only admitted the theft when the stories were not believed. She had pleaded guilty. In mitigation her lawyer argued that she was 'young in years' and of good character since her one previous offence was spent. He went on to say that his client had suffered an emotional shock in the past year, and that the circumstances were painful to relate.

> . . . A wedding that had been planned after a four-year relationship was cancelled only weeks before it was due to take place. She attempted to get away by going to Spain but came back depressed. She attempted suicide and was in . . . hospital where she has attended a clinic, her last appointment

being two weeks previous to this offence. She has been co-operative with the police.

At this point the chair magistrate interrupted:

She lied persistently until she had no option but to tell the truth.

There was no request for social inquiry reports and the defendant was fined £100 and ordered to pay £25 towards the costs of the prosecution.

In the following case the gravity of the offence, with the attendant danger of a custodial sentence, had given rise to a request for a social inquiry report which recommended a probation order. However, the magistrate did not agree with the recommendation of the report, urged by the legal representative.

Carrie Davis (aged 23) had pleaded guilty to charges of theft and decep-tion concerning cash and bank giro cheques totalling £1,264, from her place of work. The court heard that she had denied all knowledge of the event even when the cashed giro cheques aroused police suspicions and her flat was searched. As the police were about to leave empty-handed one of the officers picked up a soft toy and some of the stolen items were found inside. Only then did the defendant admit to the crime.

Addressing the magistrates her lawyer said:

This is an unfortunate case of a young woman of good record but muddled financial affairs. She is deeply troubled by what she has done and anxious to make good the money . . .

He went on to urge that a probation order be given. This met a stern response from the chair magistrate:

This is a case of deliberate repeated defrauding of an employer, a breach of trust. Normally this would merit a custodial sentence.

Anxiously the lawyer tried to find other mitigation:

I urge you to consider the report (S.I.R.), her respectable background . . .

He was interrupted by the magistrate:

Her background is no excuse, she has had every opportunity . . . On the face of it the car needed a new engine and she took the temptation . . .

The lawyer called the defendant's father as a character witness. He told the court that this behaviour was out of character and he felt ashamed.

Asked if he could explain this change of character he said he could not, and he had not noticed any change in his daughter over the preceding months. At this point the chair magistrate interrupted again to ask if the defendant could return to the family home. Her father looked doubtful and said that he would have to discuss it with his wife, since he had remarried. The magistrate withdrew the request, saying that it would not be fair to press it.

The magistrates retired to consider the sentence and this was given, on their return, with a stern reprimand.

> This was deliberate plundering which you chose not to admit . . . We do not consider that you need probation. Community Service would prevent you from taking an extra job, such as a barmaid, to repay the money.

A suspended prison sentence of three months was imposed.

Implicit, and at times explicit, in these pleas of mitigation is a model of normality. Defendants offend because their circumstances are abnormal. Defendants will reform because their circumstances will in future be normal. In the final example the defendant is presented to the court as someone who has changed her dependencies from unacceptable to acceptable ones. Cannabis and alcohol are replaced by NHS drugs and her lesbian lover by her parents as an emotional support.

Helen Dunne (aged 27) gave her address as a local mental hospital and pleaded guilty to charges of possessing and cultivating cannabis, and drunk and disorderly behaviour. Her psychiatrist took the stand and gave her history.

> (Helen) has a long history of treatment for anxiety neurosis. This takes the form of a phobia which makes her unable to travel from home unless accompanied. Alcohol and cannabis relieve the symptoms. The condition has worsened in the last few months due to the social pressure on her. The relationship with her woman friend meant that (Helen) stayed at home and kept house while her friend went to work. The relationship began to deteriorate and (Helen) became increasingly insecure, which led to the use of alcohol and suicide attempts. This relationship is now over . . .. There has been an improvement in her condition. She takes her drugs regularly. She has had to face facts now that she is no longer protected by her friend economically. Consequently she has established a better relationship with her parents . . .. They are worthy people and are prepared to help her in a way they were not when she was completely independent of them.

The psychiatrist concluded that Helen required 2 to 3 months' hospitalisation followed by out-patient treatment. The magistrates decided to give a conditional discharge of 12 months:

in view of what we've been told.

As the defendant was a woman it was seen as appropriate for her to be dependent on another for financial and emotional support, but this dependency should take place within the conventional family in which she would play the role of wife or daughter. The 'wife' role in the context of a lesbian relationship was presented as unsatisfactory and a factor contributing to her eventual breakdown. However, the problems of dependency within a conventional family unit were not discussed here or in any of the other cases seen.

Helen Dunne's problems were medicalised and she was prescribed drugs that would relieve her symptoms. By treating herself with drugs to relieve the symptoms she had failed to be an appropriate patient. Women with problems are expected to seek help from medical experts who then control the type and amount of medication to be administered. When the defendant appeared in court she had finally accepted the role that denied her all autonomy. She had achieved the status of child and patient.

The family in society and women in the family

Table 4.1, and the ensuing analysis of the arguments, indicate the extent to which discussion of the defendant within the context of the family dominates the pleas of mitigation. The predominance of the family in these pleas is an acknowledgement of the role which it plays in the socialisation and control of members of society. In this chapter I argue that the family structure which the court supports (a) involves and perpetuates the subordination of woman and (b) is necessary for the reproduction of the total society in its existing form.

It is within the family that ways of thinking and patterns of behaviour are first learned and acted out. The divisions of class, gender and race/ethnicity which characterise our society are accomplished within the distinctive life patterns of families in different sections of society. It is here that gender-roles and identities are constructed (McIntosh, 1979). Furthermore, there is a close connection between the form of the family and the socio-economic structure of society. Poster (1978) has explored this relationship using the different models of family adopted by different classes during specific historical periods. Donzelot (1979) has analysed the nature of the increasing number of interventions, made by the state, from the eighteenth century onwards, in the structuring of bourgeois and proletarian family life. The contemporary forms of family life, and the ideology supporting them, are important in the reproduction of the contemporary social structure. They also have serious implications for the position of women in society.

'Thus in reinforcing the dominant model of the family the court is reinforcing the existing relations which contribute to the structure of society. It is not necessary that there should be 'discrimination' in the pleas of mitigation for this to be achieved. Indeed, the use of the same model of the family in pleas for *both* men *and* women enhances the effectiveness of familial ideology. In its very *lack* of discrimination this familiar rhetoric reinforces the subordination of women.

The model of family evoked by the pleas of mitigation has, as its basic unit, a man and a woman, for whom the family provides a site for the exercise of social responsibility. This is also the model that underlies current legislation on family taxation and benefits. It is a model based on a sexual division of labour, and which has consequences for women in both domestic and waged labour (Finch, 1982; Land, 1978; Land, 1980; Wilson, 1977). This is discussed in Chapter 7.

Paid work for men and women, was presented in the pleas of mitigation as a laudable means of meeting family responsibilities. However, this demonstrates the inequality rather than the equality of men and women before the court. Few women could expect to earn an income sufficient to maintain themselves, or their families. Most women would be in the position of combining poorly paid waged labour with their usual domestic labour. Where the husband's wage is low, or non-existent, the woman's best efforts may still result in economic hardship – this was true in the case of Belle Waters discussed earlier in this chapter.

Pleas of mitigation frequently presented the family as an effective site of social control. It is the strength of the control operating within the family which makes it such an appropriate site for change and reformation. Defendants of either sex were frequently depicted as weak individuals open to the strong influence of a member of the opposite sex. Strong and virtuous individuals would, it was suggested, achieve the rehabilitation of the defendant within a relationship approximating to a traditional marriage. However, women by their economic dependence and social isolation within the family are the more vulnerable to coercion. As the pleas of mitigation suggest, family ties are privileged – a recognition of the necessity of strong emotional bonds in the exercise of control. Behaviour which would elsewhere result in prosecution and punishment may be excused or ignored because it occurs within the context of the family. This has detrimental consequences for the powerless in such a situation. Women may suffer a number of abuses, ranging from the withholding of an adequate share of the family wage to physical assault, or rape, and find that the law can not, or will not, intervene (O'Donovan, 1979; Dobash and Dobash, 1980). For many women the model of the family implicit in the pleas of mitigation is a model which involves economic and emotional exploitation.

The family is central to the pleas of mitigation, offered on behalf of men and women, but the emphasis on the family for defendants of both sexes is an example of a practice which seems impartial but which actually perpetuates inequality. By applying a model of family which is derived from structural inequalities courtroom practice reveals and reinforces the prevailing ideology.

In the next chapter the social inquiry reports prepared on defendants will be examined to discover how men and women are presented to the court by probation officers.

Chapter Five

Social inquiry reports

In the preceding chapter an analysis of pleas of mitigation revealed expectations concerning the relationships of men and women within the familial household. Those gender roles are part of a model of family life which is shared by other members of the court. In this chapter social inquiry reports are examined, and these confidential documents are found to confirm and extend the model of family life, and in particular the role of women, which was in use in the more public sphere of pleas of mitigation.

A social inquiry report is prepared on a defendant, by a probation officer, at the request of the magistrates. Home Office Circular No. 59/1971 says that a report should inquire into:

> ... the character, personality and social and domestic background of the accused. (Para. 11, Sec. a)

Reports are requested in situations where the magistrates require further information before deciding on a sentence, particularly if they are considering probation or custody. These reports are confidential, only the magistrates, members of the probation service, and the defendant, have a right to see them.[1] If the defendant is represented the lawyer may see the report, and may allude to the contents in a plea of mitigation.

The contents of social inquiry reports are important in a discussion of women defendants. The official statistics show that a higher proportion of women receive a conditional discharge or a probation order while a higher proportion of men receive a prison sentence. By examining social inquiry reports we can assess the influence of probation officers on the sentencing of female and male defendants; we can also learn something of the probation officers' understanding of the social situation of the defendant.

Probation Officers' Precepts and Practices

Probation officers, like social workers, use a case-work approach.

> Today the probation officer must be seen essentially as a professional case-worker, employing in a specialised field, skills which he hold in common with other social workers. (Report of the Departmental Committee on the Probation Service (1962))

This approach has traditionally focused on the families of the poor in an attempt to assess and meet their needs in an appropriate manner (Stedman Jones, 1971; Wilson, 1977). From their emergence as a professional group in the last century, until the present day, social workers have concentrated their efforts primarily on the family, and this involved focusing on the mother (Wilson, 1977; Donzelot, 1979).

As many feminists have argued, the ways in which welfare provision is constructed and administered requires that women accept responsibility for the day to day care of the home and family. Legislation is based on the assumption that the family unit will consist of a male breadwinner who provides financial support for his dependent wife and children and this has consequences for women both in the domestic sphere and the labour market (Land, 178, 1980; McIntosh, 1979). This family unit is privileged in terms of financial benefits and tax relief; it is also accorded a degree of privacy or non-intervention by the state. Within this unit gender roles and identities are constructed, and a sexual division of labour is endorsed. Because of the privacy accorded to family relationships it is impossible, in law, to ensure that the wife receives a fair proportion of the family wage,[2] or that she is adequately protected from domestic violence or rape (Dobash and Dobash, 1980; McCann, 1985). As Barrett and McIntosh (1982) have argued, this modern nuclear family unit, which is supported by contemporary social policy, is neither a natural nor a neutral arrangement. It is, furthermore, an arrangement which is of specific significance for women. The role of social workers, including probation officers, in supporting this unit is, therefore, of consequence in understanding their contribution to the continued subordination of women within our society.

Probation officers have a complex role which combines the casework approach of the social worker with the duties of an officer of the court. It is at the request of the court that probation officers prepare social inquiry reports on defendants and undertake the supervision of those given probation orders. Social inquiry reports play an important part in the judicial process; for example, there is evidence of a positive association between the recommendations they contain and the sentencing decisions made by magistrates (Thorpe and Pease, 1976). Although probation officers may argue that their role is not a punitive one, but rather, as the 1907 Probation of Offenders Act puts it, 'to advise, assist and befriend', it is indisputable that failure to co-operate with a probation officer may result in sanctions far in excess of those which could be invoked by other social workers. The function of social control is much more apparent in the role of the probation officer than it is in the role of the generic social worker. Nevertheless, initial training and professional journals emphasise the caring component of the role which the probation officer shares with other social workers. They also share a perspective which gives primacy to the ideologically dominant model of the family. Although the probation officer may have the specific task of preparing a report on, or supervising an individual defendant, while other social workers are more explicitly concerned with the family, an examination of probation officers' practices reveals a concern not just with the individual, but with the family context of the individual. Social inquiry reports, for example, describe individuals in terms of their relationships in past or present family life. Families are described with approval, implying that the cause of crime lay elsewhere or, alternatively, certain features of family life are emphasised to indicate that this is a 'problem family'. Implicitly or explicitly, probation officers present certain families as criminogenic and others as inhibitive of criminal behaviour. Like other social workers, the probation officers focus on the family life of the client, and they endorse or deny the validity of the arrangements which they encounter. The model of appropriate family life implicit in such practice, and the explanations of criminal behaviour which arise from this model, have implications which go beyond the individual defendant. From an examination of the construction of a sample of social inquiry reports, I shall argue that the practices of probation officers serve to disadvantage women by an endorsement of a model of family life which involves the oppression and exploitation of women.

Social inquiry reports at Hillbury

During the period of observation social inquiry reports were requested on 37 men and 35 women. In order to compare reports on two groups of adults to whom similar arguments might be expected to apply, the sample was confined to defendants over 21. The sample then consisted of 62 reports: 34 on women and 28 on men. The 10 officers who had written the reports and who were attached to the court were interviewed.

Most of the social inquiry reports presented at Hillbury conformed to a standard format. In the opening remarks the probation officer would indicate the number of interviews that had taken place, and where these had taken place, who else besides the defendant had been seen and what other resources had been used in the construction of the report. The report would then continue, in a series of numbered or headed paragraphs, to describe those aspects of the defendant's life which were to be presented to the magistrates. The first paragraph usually described the family of origin and the childhood circumstances of the defendant. This would be followed by a paragraph giving a brief life history covering education, employment and family circumstances since childhood. The current background was then described, particularly if it was considered relevant to the offence. The circumstances of the offence were discussed. In a final paragraph the probation officer would assess the defendant's situation and, usually, recommend a suitable sentence. The magistrates followed the probation officers' recommendations in 52 of the 59 cases in which recommendations were made, i.e. in 88 per cent of the cases.

The 62 reports were examined to discover whether the contents, or the methods used in the construction of these reports varied according to the sex of the defendant. Three major findings emerged:

(i)   While the recommendations concerning sentences corresponded to the pattern of 'leniency' for women noted in the official statistics, these were justified in terms of the offence and previous convictions, not the sex of the defendant. The sex of the defendant did not appear to directly influence the recommendation of sentence.

(ii) In the majority of cases the family circumstances of both male and female defendants were used to explain and/or excuse the offence. These accounts reinforced a sexual division of labour.

(iii) An implicit model of appropriate gender roles within the context of the family was apparent in the probation officers' differential practices when making home visits to male and female defendants.

Sentence recommendations

As Table 5.1 shows, in relation to the distribution of sentences between
men and women, the recommendations in the sample of reports correspond
to the national sentencing pattern. Probation was recommended for a
higher proportion of women, and custody for a higher proportion of men.
However, in the cases examined this could not be seen as indicative of
discrimination since the respective recommendations were made in very
different circumstances. Probation was recommended for those defendants
with few criminal antecedents, who were considered to merit help rather
than punishment. In interviews with the probation officers it became
apparent that counselling and guidance were considered appropriate to
those in situations of emotional or financial stress. The women in the
sample had fewer previous convictions than the men; even those with an
unusually high number of convictions for a woman, had fewer than those
men with a long criminal record. Most of the women were in a situation of
social isolation, compounded by domestic responsibilities and an inadequ-
ate income. Many could not pay a fine. A probation order was suggested as
an appropriate way of helping those with problems, who it was felt did not
deserve a harsh punishment, and who could not pay even a small fine. Men
in similar situations, i.e. those with few previous convictions and heavy
domestic responsibilities, received a similar recommendation. However,
few men were in such a situation. The differences in the sentences
recommended for men and women may be attributed to the different
circumstances in which they appeared before the court. The failure of
exercises in comparative sentencing to reveal instances of obvious or overt

Table 5.1 Distribution of sentence recommendations in sample of social
inquiry reports

Sentence recommended	Defendants Men	Women
Absolute or conditional discharge	7% (2)	12% (4)
Probation order	50% (14)	70% (24)
Fine	11% (2)	6% (2)
Community service order	7% (2)	6% (2)
Custodial sentence	14% (4)	3% (1)
Other	4% (1)	–
No recommendation	7% (2)	3% (1)
TOTAL	100% (28)	100% (34)

discrimination does not, however, mean that the court treats men and women equally. It is rather, an indication of the futility of employing such a narrow focus in attempting to discover the relative situations of men and women defendants. The role played by the court, and in this case the contribution of probation officers, is part of a subtle process by which women are defined as different and subordinate. It involves the use of a model of family life, a model which is rarely made explicit and is never critiqued, but which is the basis of the continued subordination of women. The use of this model will be considered below.

Family circumstances and 'causes' of crime

In the majority of cases the social inquiry report devoted much space to a discussion of the defendant's past and present family circumstances. This was equally true of reports on women and men. As Table 5.2 shows, the domestic situation was frequently used to explain the offence. In these reports probation officers described 'problem' families and situations which did not conform to the implicit norm of the 'good' family. The characteristics of the 'good' family were rarely explicit in the social inquiry reports, but they may be deduced from comments made on their absence in a 'problem' family.

The characteristics of the 'good' family presented in social inquiry reports were the same as those found in pleas of mitigation. The family was presented as the appropriate site for the discharge of social responsibility, for the socialisation of the young and for the control of all family members. Those defendants whose childhoods had not conformed to the norm were usually represented as suffering character flaws as a consequence. A large proportion of men and women were represented as offending because of a currently unorthodox domestic situation. Ten women and 4 men were described as bearing the burdens of single parenthood and/or domestic

Table 5.2 Distribution of explanations of offences in the sample of social inquiry reports

Defendants		Explanations				
		Domestic circumstances	Drug addiction	Alcoholic	Personality problem	Desire for money
Women	100% (34)	85% (29)	3% (1)	3% (1)	3% (1)	6% (2)
Men	100% (28)	82% (23)	11% (3)	4% (1)	4% (1)	–

isolation, because their partners had physically left the home or had withdrawn through alcohol, illness or inclination. In such cases, it was recognised that financial stress could lead to shoplifting, while emotional stress might lead to drink, and so to shoplifting, as the result of drink. Those who stole to supplement the family budget were represented as less culpable than those who stole for personal gain.

In their descriptions of the difficulties of single parenthood the probation officers frequently revealed their assumptions concerning appropriate gender roles within the family. Men were presented as suffering from the emotional stress of providing child-care, while women were presented as suffering the stress of economic deprivation. Of a man who, because of his wife's hospitalisation, had become responsible for the care of his 18-month-old son, the probation officer wrote:

> He can't remember taking the articles (a hairbrush and a T-shirt) because he was worried and preoccupied with getting things for the baby.

Writing of a single mother's offence the probation officer stressed the lack of money due to the lack of a male breadwinner, and described the offence as an attempt by the woman to fulfil her domestic obligations:

> . . . she went into Woolworths with no intention of stealing, saw clothes that she knew her children needed, and took them . . .

It is the conventional nuclear family which is seen to provide the social and economic support necessary for 'normal' life. Those who lack the support of a conventional family clearly are not expected to act in a conventional way. A tautological argument is engaged here: problem families may be expected to produce problem behaviour which is then attributed to the problematic nature of that particular family. The probation officer's faith in the effective influence of a conventional home-life is demonstrated by the bewilderment of an officer who could find nothing in the defendant's immediate circumstances to account for his behaviour. The defendant was a heroin addict, aged 21, who had stolen a quantity of silver and jewellery to finance his habit. In this report the use of 'appears' and 'seems' indicates the probation officer's uncertainty in the contradictory situation of a 'good' family which has not inhibited criminal behaviour.

> He comes from a successful upper-middle-class family, the youngest of two sons. He appears to have had a happy and stable background . . . This is a tragic case of a young man who has had many opportunities, but has unfortunately failed to utilise any of them, he has tremendously supportive

and understanding parents who are always ready to help and advise him. It seems that despite his parents' concern he must learn to accept responsibility for himself.

It was within the context of an unconventional family that most defendants were presented as suffering from the influences, anxieties and needs which had led to their offences. The apparent irregularity of the families of many defendants must serve to strengthen the association between an unsatisfactory home life and criminal behaviour, and conversely between the conventional nuclear family and conforming behaviour. However, social inquiry reports are not carried out on the law abiding, and traditions of privacy and loyalty make the realities of life within many families a well-kept secret. The model of the family endorsed in these social inquiry reports therefore does not necessarily correspond to the everyday domestic realities of the majority of the law-abiding population. Nevertheless, any deviation from that model, in the family circumstances of the defendant, will be proffered as a contributary factor in the offence.

The expectations and assumptions concerning family life, and especially the gender-roles within the family, became more apparent when the sample of reports was examined to discover the way in which a visit to the defendant's home was used in the construction of a report.

Making a home visit

Home visits were made only to those living in family units, particularly to those with the more serious criminal records. The proportions of men and women receiving visits were similar, i.e. 12 women and 10 men, or over a third of the defendants. In interview 6 of the 10 probation officers said that they would always make a home visit, and 4 said that they would do so if circumstances warranted it. Such circumstances ranged from the defendant's nervousness in the probation office, to an offence which was particularly related to the home. Although the probation officers did not discriminate between men and women defendants when they discussed the reasons for making a visit, the pattern that emerges from the reports suggests that to learn more about a woman it is sufficient to visit her home, but to learn more about a man, one must see the individuals who share his home. As Table 5.3 shows, visits to a woman defendant usually resulted in a description of the home, while visits to a man usually resulted in meeting a woman.

As I have outlined above, the domestic sphere is generally seen as the prime responsibility of women. My analysis of social inquiry reports shows that probation officers share this conception. Hence a home visit to a

Table 5.3 Use made of home visits by probation officers

Defendants visited		Home described	Use of visit Children seen	Meet significant adult
Women	100% (12)	83% (10)	33% (4)	8% (1)
Men	100% (10)	40% (4)	20% (2)	100% (10)

woman defendant was more likely to result in a description of the home than was a visit to a man. Of the 12 visits to women, 10 resulted in comments on the standards of comfort and cleanliness within the home. Of the 10 visits to men, only four resulted in such comments, but even in these reports the man was not held responsible for the appearance of the home. Either a description was given with no acknowledgement of the person responsible, or the reports referred to the woman of the household. In the following extract from a report on a man, aged 24, convicted of theft, the probation officer refers to the role of the defendant's mother.

... Mr Innes lives with his family in a pleasantly decorated small terraced house ... The atmosphere is warm and homely, a situation mainly attributable to Mrs Innes' motherly and compassionate feeling.

When writing reports on women defendants, probation officers often attempted to communicate a favourable impression of the women by commenting on her competence in the domestic sphere, which was judged by the appearance of her home, e.g.

She lives with her 9-year-old son, and her cohabitee in a well furnished and maintained two-bedroom flat on a pre-war council estate ... The area has a high delinquency rate and a large number of problem families. It is clear that despite this Mrs Davis has put a great deal of time and effort into making the flat into a comfortable home.

In other cases the appearance of the home would be used to suggest that the woman had emotional problems which prevented her from efficiently doing her duty. The following extract comes from a report on a man, but a comment on his wife is juxtaposed to the description of the flat in a way which both holds her responsible for, and excuses, the appearance of the home:

... The flat is clean, but crowded and untidy. Mrs Dare particularly seems to find it a stressful living situation.

In the six reports which referred to the child-care in the defendant's home, the responsibility for this was attributed to a woman. In most cases domestic labour and child-care were presented as part of the same task, e.g.

> ... Mrs Parker has high standards of personal cleanliness and this is reflected in her house and in the way her children are cared for.

The only men recognised to be responsible for child-care were single fathers, e.g.

> ... Owing to the family situation he has taken over the role of looking after the house; he prefers not to work (sic) but to concentrate on running the home ...

In these reports not only are women usually held responsible for appearance of the home and the care of the children, but the women, as individuals, are assessed by the way in which they have accomplished their domestic work. For probation officers writing reports the visit to the home may reveal much about the woman's character. Two officers discussed this aspect of their strategy in writing a report. One spoke of a case which involved a defendant, Mavis Green, aged 51, who had written a number of anonymous letters. In writing the report the probation officer deliberately used a detailed description of the defendant's home in order to communicate the defendant's obsessive character, while managing to avoid alienating a future client by direct adverse comments on her mental stability.

> It is a three-bedroomed terraced cottage decorated to a high standard and immaculately clean and tidy. There are artificial flowers everywhere. It would be difficult to find one speck of dust on the many ornaments and souvenirs filling the rooms.
> Mrs Green talks of the house with pride and the energies of all the family are channelled into the home. There is little time for small pleasures and excesses and she seems to have missed out on humour, gaiety and fun.

Commenting on that report, the probation officer told me:

> If they like you and like their report it's a good beginning. She was absolutely thrilled with that. She thought that was an absolutely wonderful report. I had described her home so carefully and obviously taken great note of it. She saw it as a sign of great approval. I'm quite sure the magistrates could see it in its sheer horror, because it was a pretty horrible room. It wasn't the social side, the class side of it. I was trying to indicate there that this was an obsessive type, neurotic and obsessive.

The second officer discussed the way in which her use of a visit to the home varied according to the sex of the defendant:

... with a married man or married woman I'd tend to home visit anyway, but a woman on her own would probably get a home visit from me more readily than a man living alone in his home ... it's something to do with the extension of the woman, seeing how she sets up her home and assuming, perhaps quite wrongly, that one would see more than visiting the man who had set up his own flat. ... With a man offender who was married I'd be more inclined to say, 'Would your wife be happy to meet me? Perhaps you could bring her in next time'. If a woman was the offender, I'd be more likely to say at the end of the first interview, 'Now it would be nice if I could visit your home' ... I'd be more likely to make a home visit and I suppose it's for the same reasons – something to do with feeling it would be illuminating to see what her nest looked like ...

The probation officer quoted above may well be articulating the expectations underlying the practices of other officers making home visits. Although the others said in interview that the sex of the defendant did not influence their strategy in preparing a report, nevertheless the pattern that emerges from the sample of reports analysed is that visits to women defendants give an opportunity for commenting on their domestic competence and judging them accordingly, while visits to men defendants give an opportunity for meeting a woman who is significant in the defendant's life. Although in interview most of the probation officers said that the home visit was used to learn more about the defendant's domestic relationships, in practice this was true of visits to men, but not women, defendants. As Table 5.3 shows, in each of the 10 reports on men a visit resulted in meeting a 'significant adult', i.e. a spouse, cohabitee or parent; out of the 12 visits made to women, only one resulted in meeting 'a significant adult'. Not only did probation officers meet the male defendant's partner, but they usually incorporated the partner's comments into the report.

Alec Burton (aged 32) pleaded guilty to causing actual bodily harm to his wife. The social inquiry report follows his account of the offence, with his wife's account:

He has been married 12 years, living locally. He says that he and his wife have been reasonably happy, but there have been upsets and rows. He claims his wife is highly strung and was in a psychiatric hospital 5 years ago. When she is upset she throws things about the house and he often comes off worst when he is trying to restrain her.

The present offence resulted when a quarrel got out of hand. She was upstairs throwing things and when she threw a fire downstairs he went up to stop her. She grabbed his hair and held on and when she toppled over he struck her to make her let go. He regrets the injuries caused. The night in police custody was a shock to him.

It is difficult to determine the cause of the quarrels. He does not drink so it was not a question of his being drunk. When he first married his wife was a Catholic and he had to agree to the children being Catholics. For the past four years she has been interested in the Jehovah's Witnesses. She goes to Bible study on Tuesdays, Wednesdays and Thursdays, and to services on Sundays. He says he cannot converse without long passages from the Bible being quoted at him.

Mrs Burton agrees that he does not drink, but he gambles. He is a good provider. Even when they were temporarily separated he always ensured they had money. But he is fussy about tidiness and it is hard to live up to his standards. She thinks his heavy handed behaviour towards her reflects what he witnessed with his own parents. He is very jealous and because of the long hours he works they have had no social life together for years. The Bible study classes are part of finding something for herself to do.

She says she does not regret calling the police as he needed to be taught a lesson and be confronted with what he was doing to her. Now she and the children want him back to make a go of the marriage.

In the report quoted above, the probation officer presents competing accounts of the same domestic situation. Since both partners were intimately concerned in the offence, it is particularly relevant to have the woman's version.

However, the wife or cohabitee may be seen as a useful source of information and insight even when she is not immediately involved in the offence. The following example concerns William Woods (aged 43) who was appearing on charges of theft and handling stolen goods. The probation officer preparing the social inquiry report found him unclear about his childhood and reticent in speaking. It was the cohabitee who helped most in the preparation of the report. The probation officer wrote:

It was from her that I gained the clearest understanding of Mr Woods' difficulties. She is far more articulate about the relationship than he is . . . Having seen Mr Woods both on his own and in the company of Miss Wright (41) I am of the opinion that he is a man who will work out his own salvation, and though polite and reasonably co-operative would be unable to respond positively under supervision.

Miss Wright is quite prepared to address the court on his recent change in attitude, and is confident that they have entered a more positive period.

In this instance not only did the cohabitee provide the probation officer with information and insight, but she offered to speak to the court on the defendant's behalf.

In other cases an interview with the spouse or cohabitee meant that the probation officer could then present the male defendant as a family man with duties and responsibilities which he was discharging within a conventional division of labour, e.g.

> Mr Vickers realises that he could get custody for this offence. He is clearly anxious to provide for Mrs Brett (his common-law wife) and her children, particularly as she is recovering from surgery and is under medical supervision.

Conclusion

These reports reveal that the man is expected to provide financially for his family, and to be concerned for their well-being, while the practicalities of child-care and housework are a woman's responsibility. However, the way in which the probation officers use the interviews with women goes beyond the mere describing of a conventional division of labour within the home. By turning to these women for comment on the situation the probation officers were acknowledging and utilising the primacy of the domestic role in the woman's life. Those who enter the home not only expect to find evidence of the woman's work, but they also expect that her domestic role will extend beyond the practical requirements of housework and child-care to the creation of a home-like atmosphere. Women are held responsible for the emotional situation in the home, and it is part of their role in the domestic sphere to encounter, and mediate with these outside influences which intrude into the home. Just as other social workers have traditionally used wives and mothers in the task of communicating with and controlling family members (Wilson, 1977; Donzelot, 1979) so the probation officers looked to women to help in the construction of social inquiry reports on men. By their professional practice in visiting a defendant's home, the probation officers place women within the domestic sphere: it is within this sphere that women are expected to account for their menfolk, it is through this sphere that they are expected to account for themselves.

The practices of probation officers in the construction of social inquiry reports reveal expectations concerning the relationships of men and women within the familial household. These gender-roles are part of a model of family life which is shared by other members of the court and recognised as a means of social control. This model is implicit *throughout* court procedures; it is apparent in pleas of mitigation and in pronouncements from the bench. The congruency of this model with the world-view of the magistrates' can be deduced from their responses to pleas of mitigation and the recommendations of social inquiry reports. In the next chapter the world-view of these ultimate decision makers will be more fully explored as they talk about their role within the court.

Chapter Six

Magistrates' talk

Obviously, magistrates play an important role in the process of summary justice, and in the reinforcement and reproduction of social divisions accomplished by summary justice. Chapter 4 described how the reactions and responses of magistrates serve to endorse or deny the validity of accounts offered by lawyers to the court. Ultimately it is the magistrates who accept or reject the arguments contained in pleas of mitigation and in social inquiry reports. They are the final arbiters in conflicting versions of the event which gave rise to the case. However, the role of magistrate is one which poses problems for many of its incumbents. By talking to magistrates I learned of the contradictions which they experienced and the solutions which they evolved – and both the contradictions and the solutions help to further define the ideologies of gender and class divisions.

Recognising a problem: Women defendants

When talking about their work, Hillbury magistrates used a model of family life which employs many of the features noted in both the public rhetoric of pleas of mitigation, and the professional discourse of social inquiry reports. Women are expected to be home-centred with responsibility for domestic labour and child-care, while men are expected to be breadwinners:

> Sometimes if there are children involved one wonders why the woman is in full-time employment. Is it economic pressure or is it social pressure, because she desperately needs to be out at work and can't stand the family life and so on. One asks more questions about a woman being in a full-time job than one does about a man, because the assumption is that a man will be in a full-time job . . . (Magistrate (woman))

This traditional division of labour also involves a hierachy while the woman is held responsible for the running of the home, she is accountable to the man:

> I think something is said about the person in the home by their physical circumstances. If a place is left dirty, continually, at an unacceptable level, that tends to say . . . something . . . I think it is important to differentiate between what it says about the person and what it says about the person's problems . . . with a woman with a number of children and a husband in trouble . . . possibly the marriage itself in trouble, a dirty home and difficulties of that nature might present a picture of depression in her rather than the fact that she is a slut as such . . . most people on the bench look to the woman to maintain the standards of the home . . . (but) it says something about the man – the fact that he is indifferent to, or can tolerate, or *does nothing to encourage an alteration of these standards*. (Magistrate (woman). Emphasis added.)

However, when talking about the family lives of defendants, magistrates were eager to distinguish between middle-class and working-class defendants. Gender-role was nearly always related to social class:

> . . . you get a little more shock with some of the women when you know their background – when you see somebody who's really quite well dressed and obviously fairly cultured, it is a shock, even if you realise right from the start that it's a cry for help, because of some emotional disturbance. It's still a shock. But one can understand if it's a mother with several kids and she hasn't any money and she pinches a pair of shoes or the basic foods. (Magistrate (woman))

Typically, that magistrate attributes gender-related motives to both women – the middle-class woman is recognised as emotionally disturbed, the working-class woman is caring for her children. However, the distinction between middle-class and working-class motivations is also a distinction between non-criminal and criminal behaviour. If a woman is middle class, it is much more difficult for the magistrate to believe that the actions are those of a criminal. For many magistrates any similarity between the defendant and themselves poses a problem:

> One woman, I remember, who'd never had any form of criminal background before, and had gone out on a major shoplifting spree, and in 24 hours had taken a mass of stuff, a really large amount of property – and one couldn't conceive what sort of brainstorm had brought this behaviour on to a woman of normal middle-class respectable background. (Magistrate (woman))

Not only motivation, but also the judicial response has to be assessed in the context of the defendant's social position. One magistrate explained why, in her view, probation was not suitable for upper middle-class defendants:

> Very often a probation officer going into a home may be able to sort out an awful lot of problems, but there's a – I don't want to sound patronising because I don't feel it and I think the probation officers are marvellous. I think there's a very slight problem if you put them into an upper middle-class home – the way the upper middle-class home will regard the probation officer would work against the system, and if I, personally, could fine a woman in that position I would rather do that and get it out of the way, finished, clean cut, rather than risk putting a probation officer in her home. That might be a continuous shame on her.

The magistrate then illustrated her point with the following example taken from her recent experience:

> . . . I had a shoplifter of that sort, a very upper middle-class lady, and we really wanted to give her probation, but she was already having psychiatric treatment, privately, and her husband had walked out on her anyway so she was alone at home, so there was no shame in bringing a probation officer in, but it was her first offence, it was shoplifting and in the end we said, 'We'll slap a fine on her because if she's going to reappear, she's going to reappear again quite quickly and probation will still be suitable'. But we agonised long over that because probation seemed very suitable, clearly the probation officers thought it was suitable too, and were only too keen to get in and help her. But in the end we decided the other way.

The ready attribution of criminal motivation or the imposition of social work surveillance are, apparently, more appropriate for the working-class defendant. The origins of the probation service in nineteenth-century missionary work with the poor seem, here, a century later, to be an influence on the perception of magistrates dealing with middle-class offenders. Social work was, and apparently still is, something that the middle class do on behalf of the working class. When discussing their own role, most magistrates expressed a concern with helping those in need and the relative positions of middle-class magistrates and working-class defendants serve to perpetuate this nineteenth-century model. This was recognised by one magistrate, who had been appointed because of his work in a trade union. Speaking of his middle-class colleagues he said:

> They've got sympathy for the less well-off, the less fortunate. They've got sympathy but they tend to view them as, not the criminal class, but – 'us and them'.

Reproducing a hierarchy

In the interviews, magistrates frequently focused on the issue of social class. Not only was gender discussed in relation to social class, but the contrast between the social class of those on the bench and those in the dock was a matter of expressed concern. For the magistrates their own position of privilege posed a problem, but it also offered a solution. In rationalising the conflict which they experienced the magistrates drew on dominant ideological explanations of the relationship of rich and poor, powerful and powerless.

To understand the dilemma faced by many magistrates it is necessary to consider the source of their authority. In a system of amateur justice they are appointed because of their local expertise. As one writer on the subject says:

> The declared policy of each Lord Chancellor since 1945 has been to make sure that each bench is a microcosm of the local community within which it operates . . . (Skyrme, 1979:62)

However, despite attempts by the Lord Chancellor's Office[1] to make the bench more representative, magistrates are still drawn largely from the middle class. Hillbury is no exception, of the sample of 30 magistrates interviewed, only one had the status of a working-class member of the bench. The majority were professional or business men and women, or women married to men whose income enabled them to engage in voluntary work without causing economic hardship to the family. (See Table A.2 in the Research Appendix.)

The dominance of middle-class magistrates may not be the intention of the Lord Chancellor's Office, but it is almost inevitable given the present system. Magistrates must be able to attend court once a fortnight for at least half a day. To do this a magistrate must have a degree of control in his or her employment which is found more usually in middle-class than in working-class occupations. The difficulties which are faced by those with less autonomy in their work were explained by a working-class magistrate:

> Can you afford the time? You're not paid so there's loss of earnings and you could be out of pocket. What employer wants you away every week or fortnight? It doesn't do your promotion chances any good. Most of the nationalised industries give 18 days per year paid leave, so I'm able to take my half day and gamble that I'll be back at work by one or two (o'clock) . . . . I use up a lot of my annual holidays – it can cost me up to a week of my holidays. But I don't mind because I think it's worthwhile. (Magistrate (man))

The same magistrate was conscious of the difference between his life and that of many of his fellow magistrates; and, furthermore, of the difference in life-styles between the majority of magistrates and the majority of defendants. Speaking of his colleagues at Hillbury he said:

> I don't think there's anyone who's just got up that morning and done the washing before she comes to court. She might have taken the children to school in the Volvo, and dropped them off, and come quite prepared to sit and talk to me about the week or fortnight ago that they were ski-ing in Austria. Then they go into court to see someone on social security, one-parent family, in a council flat.

An unease at the social distance between those in the dock and those on the bench was also expressed by the more socially privileged magistrates.

> I do feel on the whole, that my style of life – I can't compare it with most of the people that go through the courts, because they come from a lower strata, on the whole, and it's difficult to know how their life is and how it's affected them. Some of them have had a raw deal to start off with . . . one's life is very easy and you don't see how people who've been out of work or poor people live. You don't come across that, which, I just feel it's hard to go and sit in court and see people who've had perhaps a more difficult time. (Magistrate (woman))

However, that magistrate resolved the dilemma by deciding that it is only members of her own social class that are prepared to do the work involved in being a magistrate:

> Most of the people who do commit offences wouldn't want to be a magistrate. They don't want the responsibility.

Having expressed concern that social distance prevents her from knowing much about the majority of defendants, the magistrate then draws on common-sense understandings of the attitudes and motivations of working-class men and women. The solution to the problem posed by experience is achieved within the framework of the dominant ideology. The concept of 'us and them' referred to earlier can be found underlying many of the comments made by magistrates. Most magistrates said that voluntary and political work in the community, combined, in some cases, with managerial experience at work, made them familiar with the problems of the people who appeared in the dock.

> I've had children, I've got grand-children. I've had local government experience, and working (voluntarily) in Lambeth – a different world from here – Brixton with their multi-racial community and with all the problems you can possibly think of and I think this gives you some understanding of the lives people lead who are not – well this is a very middle-class area, and the pressures are very different from what they are if you're a West Indian of about 16 with two babies in a bed-sitter in a top floor in Brixton. (Magistrate (woman))

Officially magistrates are selected as a representative cross-section of the local community; in practice, this is rarely achieved. For some this clearly posed a problem concerning their right to sit on the bench, to judge and sentence others. Several mentioned the secrecy surrounding selection as a factor which further contributed to a sense of unease about their role. The strongest criticism came from a working-class magistrate; however, the points which he makes were reiterated by others:

> When someone comes, they suddenly appear on the bench. You don't know where he comes from unless he's known to you personally. Someone must have said 'We need someone like you on the bench'. He filled in an application form and went before a selection committee which is comprised of your local bench – four or five people. Now who they are I don't know and I certainly didn't vote for them.[2]

While he respected his colleagues that magistrate was very disturbed by what he perceived as bias and secrecy in the constitution of the bench:

> I feel that I respect the integrity of everybody on the bench, but I'm sure that more justice would be seen to be done if they said 'Let's have it like Inner London'.[3] Here were have a secret society – you don't know who's on the selection committee, who's been put forward, certainly not how they're chosen. We've got solicitors' wives ad lib – middle-class, well off; people who've got their own businesses – shops; hardworking – I respect their

integrity. They're intelligent people, but I don't think they're necessarily the best people to judge everybody else in the community.

Some local benches have been known to respond to that kind of criticism by advertising for working-class magistrates in the local press. However, even if selection committees are willing or eager to change the social composition of the bench, structural factors will still impede applications from working-class men and women. Without job security and a degree of control over the timing of work and attendance at the work-place, it is impracticable, if not impossible, to sit on the bench. And so the gap between the judging and the judged continues. The magistracy is dominated by middle-class men and women who have neither the mandate of the elected representative nor the recognised qualifications of the professional. They experience a contradiction in being in authority while having little to justify their authority. In a democratic society they hold a position of power by virtue of their social status.

It is interesting to notice how the magistrates describe above 'solve' the problem of bias in the composition of the local bench. While one middle-class woman decides that working-class people are not prepared to do the work of a magistrate, another decides that her voluntary work among working-class people qualifies her for the role. Both women draw on an ideologically dominant view of the relationship between a benevolent middle class and a feckless working class. The development of this attitude, from its early manifestations in Victorian charitable activities, has been chronicled and analysed (Stedman Jones, 1971; Wilson, 1977). Faced with the growing poverty and demoralisation of the urban slums, middle-class men and women embarked on programmes aimed at not only relieving hardship but at raising the moral standards of an apparently degenerate people. Structural oppression was 'explained' as moral inequality; the superiority of the powerful was attributed to their praiseworthy characters and actions, while the powerless could be categorised into the deserving and the undeserving poor. The attitude survives as a justification of inequality. If magistrates rationalise their situation by evoking tenets of the dominant ideology, which depict social superiority as moral superiority, it is not surprising that middle-class defendants cause surprise and bewilderment, and a readiness to doubt the criminal status of their acts.

For many magistrates the position of authority which they hold within the court is an endorsement of their position of superiority within a stratified society. By playing a role in the process of summary justice the magistrates not only contribute to the reinforcement of class and gender divisions, they also reinforce their own social position. Any challenge to the authority or dignity of the court may be seen as a challenge to the structures, both social and judicial, which accord the magistrates their privileged position. This was revealed when the Hillbury magistrates discussed their attitudes towards the other major participants in the process of summary justice – to defendants, lawyers, probation officers and police officers.

Defendants

Respect and deference were expected from other members of the court, especially from defendants. All but two of the magistrates told me that they considered that the defendant's demeanour was an influential factor when determining guilt:

> ... we've got to decide, very often, on facts which are in dispute, and somebody's telling a lie. Obviously demeanour gives us a great indication of who is telling the lie. (Magistrate (man))

and when deciding on a punishment:

> I must admit to a very high degree of bias on this. I am affected at all times by people's appearance and demeanour. I am influenced by a person who takes the proceedings of the court sufficiently seriously that they dress in an appropriate way and they behave in an appropriate way, and they regard it as a serious matter. If by their whole demeanour, appearance and manner they regard it as a bit of a joke, or something not terribly serious, then, in a sense a feeling rises in me – 'My God, we'll show them that this is a serious matter'. So yes, someone who appears to take it seriously I would tend to be more lenient towards. (Magistrate (man))

Physical attributes were not recognised as important, but appropriate attitudes were:

> ... I think I can successfully cut out of mind altogether what I would call the purely superficial aspects like smartly dressed or shabbily dressed, and clean or dirty, and I hope I can put out of my mind the superficial like – is it an attractive 21-year-old girl, or a very unattractive 50-year-old man, and I suspect I can't entirely put out of my mind what I would call deliberate signals of disapproval of authority in general. I find it very difficult not to get a little annoyed by the chap who is manifestly hanging around in the dock with his hands in his pockets, and leaning over chewing gum, and all the rest of it. Although I do my best not to, to the extent that I perhaps tend to be more tolerant of some of these things than some other people, than indeed some of the court clerks would be. (Magistrate (man))

Social control in a democratic society is justified by an appeal to the legal authority of the rules, the rule-makers and the rule-enforcers. Failure to recognise that authority constitutes a challenge to the court and may be met by an assertion of the power which resides there.

Most magistrates commented on the importance of an appropriate demeanour in the defendant, some were also sensitive to challenges to their authority, perceived in the actions of other court personnel.

Lawyers

The presence of lawyers could be seen as an inhibiting factor in the magistrates' task of determining innocence or guilt.

> ... on minor matters, I have to say, I would very often prefer that they (defendants) were not represented at our level. I think I would rather hear from the person themselves than from some clever solicitor who's concerned only to get them off – that's his job – and not necessarily with justice being done, and I take a slightly jaundiced view of a lot of solicitors because of that aspect. I'd much rather have them face to face and ask them questions myself. (Magistrate (man))

The presence of lawyers reduces the hearing to a battle between skilled combatants, in which the one who wins may be the most competent but not necessarily on the side of right. This undermines the rhetoric of justice – that each individual is equal before the law, and justice will be determined on the merits of the case. Some magistrates stated that it was possible for the unrepresented defendant to have a fair hearing. This was the opinion of those senior magistrates who had given many years of their lives to the magistracy, and who firmly believed in its concept of amateur justice. It was also the opinion of the senior clerks who had confidence in their ability to lucidly explain the procedure and conduct the court fairly. However, the majority of clerks and magistrates held a different opinion. They considered that the realities of courtroom interaction put the defendant at a disadvantage.

> ... it makes the clerk's job a lot easier, the solicitor will obviously have discussed the matter with his client beforehand. He knows where the strengths and weaknesses are, so, hopefully, the solicitor is leading the questioning in some sort of logical line. It makes the defendants happier if they've got someone. It's like a game really, if someone knows the rules and you don't, then it's easier to let the one that knows the rules play. (Clerk (woman))

> I'm rather sad when people say they can handle the case themselves, because you know jolly well, when they're up against prosecution, they can't. (Magistrate (woman))

There is also the fact that the defendant's inexperience may impede the efficient progress of the case:

> Defendants should be represented as often as possible. It's easier for the court, easier for the defendant, easier for the bench. (Magistrate (woman))

Probation Officers

Probation officers are members of the court who, like lawyers, could be perceived as a challenge to the autonomy of the magistrates. Some magistrates expressed annoyance at probation officers' recommendations concerning a suitable sentence.[4] The following comment is based on an erroneous[5] conception of the construction of a social inquiry report; nevertheless, it may be influential on the speaker's practice, and he obviously does not feel that he is alone in his opinions.

> something that gets everybody's back up is that they presume to make some sort of recommendation – 'I feel that if you were disposed towards probation they are quite suitable'. And they've heard no more than we have. They haven't told us any more and in the few moments that they've spent with the defendant, they're prepared to make some form of judgment. We may have spent an hour or two hours in court listening to all the facts. Now the social inquiry report is based on two half hour periods talking only to the defendant and the arresting officer. (Magistrate (man))

Others were less hostile but emphasised their own authority in matters of sentencing.

> . . . they can only put forward suggestions, it's down to us what we do. Most of the time we probably think they're right and we follow, but sometimes we don't for jolly good reasons, something they hadn't thought about. (Magistrate (woman))

Most magistrates spoke as though the selection of the relevant facts, from the welter of events that constitute an individual's life, was unproblematic.

The probation officers realise that what we want to know is what they can find out, and although we appreciate, and their comments are extremely useful and helpful, they recognise that we like to make our own assessment on the facts they present to us. (Magistrate (woman))

Magistrates may feel a need to assert their authority in the face of a reality in which they usually follow the probation officer's recommendation (Thorpe and Pease, 1976). Not all were defensive, some openly admittd their debt to the probation officers.

The more facts from responsible people like the probation service, and I think, too, some of their conclusions that they suggest are important, because I think perhaps in dealing with this sort of person they're more skilled than we are. This is their job, they're dealing with these people all the time. (Magistrate (man))

The attitude of magistrates towards the probation officers tended to be influenced by the degree of social and professional interaction which occurred. This was noticed by Burney in her study (1979:173). At Hillbury many of the magistrates who expressed respect for the probation service were the ones who had served on the Probation and After-care Committee. Such experience also allowed the magistrates to distinguish between different probation officers.[6]

... one gets to know their particular specialities, where they do know an awful lot of a family or a family situation. One knows how far one can rely utterly on what they say and recommend rather than some of the others. (Magistrate (woman))

... We do have meetings, through the Probation and After-care Committee joint meetings, joint social affairs where probation officers and social workers are invited, and they get to know us, and we get to know them, and through that one gains an impression of any newcomers, what sort of people they are, what sort of report they'd make. (Magistrate (man))

Far fewer magistrates were critical of probation officers than were critical of lawyers, but those who expressed their aversion were also the ones who admitted that they had little interaction with the members of the probation service.

There are probation meetings. I came to one which was fairly hostile – I can't remember whether it was social services or probation services – I have the feeling it was probation, but I'm not sure, but it was quite hostile. (Magistrate (man))

The magistrate quoted above was very critical of the probation service, but his personal contact did not extend beyond one meeting, and he was unsure about the constituency of the meeting.

Police

Of those magistrates who mentioned the police only two were slightly critical in their comments. The others spoke approvingly of the conduct of the police in court, and admitted to being influenced by their presentation of a case:

> In general one is, of course, influenced by this, whatever the sex of the person, if the police officer gives a sympathetic review. He says 'They were co-operative and I understand there are circumstances'. (Magistrate (woman))

The lack of criticism of the police could be attributed to the fact that the magistrates perceived no challenge to their authority in the actions of the police. This may not be true of the magistrates' perceptions of other court personnel.

Justices of the peace are essentially high-status amateurs.[7] During the course of their duties on the bench they encounter a number of professionals who have received more training but enjoy less authority within the hierarchy of the court. Police officers,[8] probation officers,[9] solicitors [10] and barristers [11] are all groups whose members have received a training of a length and intensity greater than that of the magistrates. The group with the least amount of such professional training, is also one which aroused the least comment from the magistrates, and most of the comments were favourable. Police officers are also likely to be perceived as socially inferior and so less likely to challenge the status conscious magistrates. Probation officers and lawyers receive a much longer training and both groups consider their members to be professionals. Members of both groups may advance arguments which are derived from skills not shared by the magistrates and which contravene the magistrates expectations. The magistrates may feel vulnerable. Their authority is not supported by either professional qualifications or the democratic vote of an electorate. Their authority is derived solely from an appointment, via a process shrouded in secrecy, to a body constituted mainly from the upper strata of society, and charged with the duty of enforcing the rules which ensure the continuance of that society in its present form. In perceiving and describing challenges to the authority of the magistrates, these men and women did not distinguish between the authority of the court and their personal authority.

Conclusion

Many of the differences and divisions which mark contemporary Britain are represented and reinforced by the routines of summary justice. In this the magistrates play an important part.

The Hillbury bench consists of almost equal numbers of men and women. There are 44 (47 per cent) women and 40 (53 per cent) men. The sample selected consisted of 13 (43 per cent) women and 17 (57 per cent) men. In this sample all the men described their paid employment when asked about their full-time occupation. Even the retired men classified themselves in this way, as 'retired architect' or 'retired accountant'. The majority (16) of the men were professional or business men. The majority of the women (8) described themselves as housewives, two added that they had part-time jobs outside the home. Those women who described their full-time occupations in terms of their paid employment were, for the majority (4), engaged in activities associated with their gender role of caring for children or concerned with the home. The one exception was the senior civil servant, who was also the only single woman in the sample. Any panel of magistrates in any Hillbury courtroom is likely to consist of a mixture of men and women who, in their daily lives, live out a traditional gender role. Describing her own and her colleagues' attitudes, one magistrate said:

> I don't think men always understand women, I think women, it sounds a bit arrogant, I think women understand men a bit better. They are less . . . well a chap goes to the office, meets the same people all the time. It's very much a set routine. We have to do a lot more giving and taking and fitting in and getting on with different types of people. I think that helps, a lot, to have more understanding.

She saw male magistrates to have different strengths. Although she is a woman with a home and family of her own, she said:

> If it's anything financial I'm lost. I think 'Thank God I'm with a man who knows what he's talking about' – that's if I'm in the domestic courts, because with finance or maintenance – oh, terrible! (Magistrate (woman))

These gender-roles are, however, the gender-roles of members of the middle class. Hillbury bench, like so many benches, cannot be said to constitute a representative cross section of the local population. What it does constitute is a microcosm of middle-class society. Most of the men practise their professions and run their businesses. Most of the women have paid help with domestic duties and spend much time on voluntary community work.

Within the court the social hierarchies of society are enacted. Typically, middle-class magistrates sit in authority over working-class defendants; and when the defendant has the social attributes of a magistrate the anomaly is cause for comment.

Within the court the magistrates enjoy a position of power and privilege, corresponding, usually, to their social positions out of court. While many of these men and women may be personally well suited to the task of dispensing summary justice, it is also true that many of them continue to be beneficiaries of the social system which is supported by the courts of justice. They are, structurally, well suited to their role in the process of social reproduction. This role is played effectively through the magistrates' responses to gender and class. In their attitude to the family life of the defendants, magistrates endorse the gender divisions which form the basis of pleas of mitigation and social inquiry reports. By their response to the social differences between defendants and members of the bench, magistrates endorse their own position of legal, moral, and social superiority, and, in so doing, they endorse the hierarchical structures of society.

Chapter Seven

Summary justice and familial ideology

The question of equality

From observations at Hillbury Magistrates' Court, documentary analysis, and interviews with magistrates and probation officers I concluded that when men and women appear in similar circumstances, charged with similar offences, they receive similar treatment. These findings, based on a qualitative methodology, correspond to the findings of a recent study which used a quantitative methodology. Farrington and Morris (1983), whose work was discussed in Chapter 2, controlled for offence and previous conviction when they examined the sentencing of men and women at Cambridge City Magistrates' Court. They, too, found that the sex of the defendant was not a direct influence on the sentence received. Those who have attempted to address this issue solely in terms of the surface similarities between cases may find that there are no obvious differences in the treatment of male and female defendants. However, the limitations of this approach are discussed in Chapters 1 and 2, where it is argued that the question of equality is problematic and not easily resolved. Legal rhetoric may assert that all are equal before the law; however there is a contradiction in the promise of equality by the courts of a society in which members

are obviously unequal in other respects, e.g. wealth, resources and expertise.

In discussions of equality it is all too easy to equate formal equality with
actual equality. I have argued that the process of law is concerned not with
equality but with a ratification of the *status quo*. This position is exem-
plified in the work of Carlen (1976) and McBarnet (1981) which was
discussed in Chapter 3. Both authors reveal the class bias of law, and law
enforcement, in courts which claim to treat all equally. Now, just as class
has been recognised as a significant factor for the way in which the law
operates, so it can be argued that gender is also relevant. It is, I would
suggest, naive to assume that equality is possible within a system based on
inequality, whether one is considering class or gender differences. The
courts, in operating to endorse and reinforce the *staus quo*, must endorse
and reinforce the divisions of class and gender upon which the *status quo* is
based.

The question of inequality

In the present study it is argued that Hillbury Magistrates' Court is
involved in social control and cultural reproduction in three ways. Firstly,
the formal rules of society are upheld by the public trial of offenders.
Secondly, the hierarchies of a class divided society are reinforced by the
interactions of middle-class magistrates and working-class defendants.
Thirdly, the gender divisions which characterise the society are reinforced
by the ideology of family life which permeates judicial discourse.

The dominant ideology of a society is made up of the models of normality
by which people in that society live their daily lives. These models
legitimate and justify the divisions and hierarchies within that society.
Furthermore, they are accepted by many who derive no material benefit
from them, and for whom they are a source of continuous oppression and
exploitation. How this acceptance is accomplished – how the consent of the
dominated to the world-view of the dominant is achieved – is of major
concern to sociologists. This world-view, with its perceptions, explanations
and justifications is promulgated by the institutions controlled by the
dominant classes, particularly those controlled by the state, including the
legal system.

Althusser (1971) differentiates between Ideological State Apparatuses
(I.S.A.s) and Repressive State Apparatuses (R.S.A.s). The I.S.A.s include
institutions, such as the mass media and the education system, which
perform a role in the social control of society by communicating the
dominant ideology. The R.S.A.s, such as the police and the armed forces,
are more directly coercive, and are brought into situations where the

I.S.A.s have failed. The legal system is coercive of the defendant, but it also operates at the level of ideology. As courts are public places the judicial process communicates with an audience beyond those immediately involved in prosecution and defence.

Within the dominant ideology of contemporary British society, women are the subordinate members of each class, and are primarily domestic in their concerns. The model of the family within this ideology is one which, despite the involvement of the state in its support, is justified by the claim that it is a 'natural' form of organisation. In this work my aim has been to demonstrate how this model of the family is reflected in, and reinforced by, the process of summary justice. Within Hillbury Magistrates' Court we can see the material reality of the dominant ideology. The attitudes and assumptions of those involved in the social construction of justice are revealed through the language of the judicial process. In spoken argument and written document, members of the court employ a model of social normality at the centre of which is the family. At Hillbury a common model was used by lawyers in public discussions, and by probation officers in confidential reports; and this model was endorsed by the magistrates in their responses. Through family circumstances the defendant was explained, excused, and given hope for the future. Other aspects of life, such as paid employment or health, were discussed in relation to the family. This model has implications for the social control of all defendants, but it is particularly oppressive of women.

In the sections that follow, this chapter will proceed to examine the consequences for women of the ideologically dominant model of the family. I will discuss (a) the poverty and (b) the isolation which result from the prevalence of this model throughout society, and (c) the role played by this model in the system of summary justice.

Women and poverty

The model of the family which is implicit in the courtroom discourse is one which is supported by tradition, policy and legislation in a way which has implications for the position of women both within and beyond the family. Welfare policy is based on the assumption that the family unit will consist of a male breadwinner who provides the financial support for his dependant wife and children, and a woman who is primarily concerned with the caring and nurturing of the family through her domestic labour. Men may expect to earn a 'family wage', since it is assumed that their earnings provide for others. Most women, however, find that the jobs available to them do not offer similar rates of pay. The average full-time wage for a woman in 1983 was 72 per cent of a man's wage. Women in part-time work who constitute two-fifths of the female labour force, are even worse off. Their hourly wage in 1983 was, on average, 57 per cent of the hourly rate paid to men in full-time work (Kahn, 1985:81). As part-time workers such women have fewer rights to sick pay, holiday pay, or pensions. In an examination of recent legislation and practice, Peggy Kahn (1985) concludes that employment law is based on, and reinforces, a sexual division of labour:

> ... much employment law and many collective agreements are predicated upon the male worker, a worker with few domestic responsibilities in full-time employment at a unionised work-place. There is little effective regulation of the sort of work women manage to undertake, work that is often part-time and reflects women's family roles. Where women are excluded from employment, the law does little to encourage integration of the work-force. (Kahn, 1985:79)

The Equal Pay Act may be invoked only where men and women receive different remuneration for doing the same job. Because of this commitment to uniformity of treatment the Act is ineffective in challenging the low pay received by the majority of women concentrated in a narrow range of jobs. Over 75 per cent of employed women work in the service sector, in jobs which can not, under the law, be compared to jobs done by men. Furthermore, women are poorly paid not only in relation to men but also in terms of accepted definitions of adequate earnings, i.e. £92.70 per week in 1982/3 or less than £104.31 per week to support a two-child family (Khan, 1985:85). And the situation is getting worse not better since the passing of the equal rights legislation.

The low wages available to women mean that for many working-class women economic independence is not possible; marriage becomes necessary if they are to move away from the parental home (McRobbie, 1978:107). Even within marriage the woman has no assurance that she will receive a proportion of the wage which is intended for the upkeep of a man's wife and children. The distribution of resources within the household is not only under-researched, but is subject to the traditions of privacy on matters concerning the internal management of the familial household. Existing research indicates that many families live in poverty despite the apparent adequacy of the breadwinner's wage (Pahl, 1980). Moreover, while a married couple are living together there is no effective legal provision for the enforcement of maintenance (O'Donovan, 1979:141).

The domestic responsibilities of marriage bring long hours of work for most women.[1] Child-care and housework are assumed to be a woman's work even if she has paid employment outside the home (Young and Willmott, 1973). Consequently, the choice facing many women is either the 'double shift' of paid employment and domestic labour, or the isolation and lower income of full-time housework.

Poverty is, for many women, the result of legislation and provision based on the concept of a family wage. Women's earning power in the labour market is reduced, and the money that they can earn usually goes directly into the household finances. While many men expect a part of their wages to be used for their personal spending, most women do not receive a similar personal allowance from the family wage, nor retain one from their own earnings (Pahl, 1980). Women are expected to provide their domestic labour without personal monetary reward.[2]

Women and isolation

State policies and social conventions which construct women's domestic role and economic dependency, also contribute to their isolation and the consequences of such isolation. Many women have neither the money nor the time for leisure pursuits outside the home. A lack of provision[3] for communal child-care and domestic work involves many women in long hours of isolated, repetitive, low status work (Brunsden, 1978; Hobson, 1978). The most obvious results of this are the high rates of depression among housebound women. Depression is more likely among women involved full-time in housework than it is among unmarried women and married women with jobs outside the home (Procek, 1981; Brown *et al.*, 1975; Gavron, 1966). The housewife is vulnerable to poverty and depression. Poverty may be attributed to her structural definition as an economic dependant, but the roots of depression are more complex and obscure. Depression may best be understood in the context of the psychological vulnerability arising from isolation.

Isolation is not just the result of the conditions of domestic labour, it is also a consequence of prevailing attitudes on the privacy of the home. The home is frequently represented as a sanctuary from the hurly-burly of the outside world (Lasch, 1977). Since the isolated housewife does not take part in this hurly-burly her opportunities for social interaction are reduced. If her friends are not welcome when her husband is at home she may find herself deprived of company both in work and leisure, in a way that her husband, with access to work-mates and public houses, is not. In the study discussed in Chapter 1 of the formal and informal modes of control experienced by a group of women prisoners, Pat Carlen presents the social isolation of many housewives through the words of her respondents, who describe how their husbands forbid their wives' friends to visit the family home but insist on their own right to go out leaving their wives with only young children for company during the evening or at the weekend.

I used to get rid of anyone who was in the house before he came in from work (even though my name was in the rent book) because I knew he could just be quite blunt and say 'Come on, out you go' . . . (Carlen, 1983:53)

Well, to tell the truth he didn't have as much time with Flora (the baby) as I would have liked him to. He still jumped about with his pals . . . But as far as he was concerned I was the mother and my place was in the home . . . He was out quite a lot you know, so it was just me and her in the house. (Carlen, 1983:46)

As Carlen's respondents illustrate, the concept of the privacy of the home is related to the hierarchy within the family. Control in this situation resides with the man; he may allow or refuse to have others in the home. In this, and other matters, he may impose on his wife a code of conduct that he himself does not follow. Within the home the power differential makes the woman vulnerable to forms of control ranging from subtle manipulation to physical coercion; and such control is made effective by prevailing attitudes on the privacy of the home.

Close personal networks are an effective form of control because of the intensity of the emotional involvements. In interaction with others, men and women construct definitions of themselves and their situations. Those isolated from other social contacts which might offer alternative views are most vulnerable to control by family members (Bell and Newby, 1976). Isolation may exacerbate a woman's psychological dependence on the family members, particularly on those most significant in her life. While her children spend time at school and her husband spends time at work or in the pub, the woman is confined to the same place for work and leisure. She is restricted in her physical movement, and in her opportunities for gaining a different perspective on herself and her situation; her situation has been compared to imprisonment (Dalh and Snare, 1978).

Subtle forms of control are to be found within many families where the wife acquiesces to her status and accepts the legitimacy of her husband's authority. However, the pattern of control is most obvious within those relationships where the man physically assaults the woman. Dobash and Dobash (1980) argue that marital violence can be understood only in the context of the hierarchy within the marital relationship. Violence is not simply the result of a quarrel, it arises in situations where the husband feels the need to assert his dominant status. A minor incident may provoke a ferocious attack when the husband perceives such an incident as a challenge to his authority or a neglect of his wishes (Dobash and Dobash, 1980:97–123).

Marital violence reveals, in its most extreme form, the inter-relationship between the patterns of social control within the family and the traditions of privacy accorded to family life. These traditions are endorsed by both the law, and the agents of law enforcement. At the level of law enforcement, police are reluctant to intervene between a husband a wife (Dobash and Dobash, 1980; McCann, 1985). At the level of the law in statute, rape, usually recognised as one of the most serious crimes, is not even an offence when the wife is the victim of the husband.

The quandary posed by the conventional family structure is that it allows a disproportionate amount of power to the man; if he wishes he may wield this power tyrannically. Obviously, many husbands do not refuse to contribute to domestic work, withhold the family wage, beat their wives or force them to have sexual intercourse against their will. People are constrained not determined by social structures, and while there is the potential for exploitation and misery within the commonly accepted model of the family, there is also the possibility of alternative arrangements, either within or beyond the conventional structures. However, these possibilities may be explored only if a man relinquishes the power given to him by statute, policy and tradition.

Meanwhile, the model of the family which prevails in contemporary ideology – portrayed in the mass media and supported by policy and legislation – involves a husband/father in the economic support of his wife and children, and a wife/mother involved in full-time domestic labour and child-care. This unit is privileged in law and tradition. It is the place of relaxation and recuperation after work; it is also the site of socialisation for the next generation. It enjoys a degree of privacy and non-intervention that is not to be found in other spheres of work and leisure. However, it is also a model which involves a structured hierarchy which disadvantages women both at home and in the labour market, and renders them vulnerable to exploitation and oppression.

The family and the court

The dominant model of the family is one which is reflected in, and reinforced by, courtroom discourse. It was implicit in pronouncements from the bench, pleas of mitigation, and probation officers' reports. The family context of the defendant formed the basis of much courtroom discussion. In discussing these contexts the court officials did more than describe a variety of domestic arrangements, they revealed their assumptions concerning the appropriate ways in which families should be organised, and their expectations concerning the results of such organisation.

The dominant features of the model of the family in use by the court are discussed in Chapters 4 and 5. In Chapter 4 pleas of mitigation are analysed to reveal the family as the major site for an individual's discharge of social responsibility. By acting appropriately as a family member a man or woman could demonstrate responsibility and respectability. Paid employment was seen as a means of contributing to the family, rather than the wider society.

The family was also recognised as a site of social control. The hope of rehabilitation was seen to lie with the defendant's role within the family. The intensity of emotional involvement, by which such control is effected, is heightened by the traditions of privacy and non-intervention in matters related to family life. In recognition of the privileged status of familial interactions, disputes and assaults were mitigated when they occurred within the context of the family.

The family was represented as an enduring unit which involves, primarily, a man and a woman. Expectations concerning the division of labour between the man and the woman were apparent from the social inquiry reports, and are discussed in Chapter 5. Comments on the material condition of the home attributed the responsibility for housework to the woman, either to the defendant or the defendant's wife or mother. Women were also held responsible for the care and appearance of the children. For the male defendant, children were presented as a responsibility to be met by the provision of an adequate income. In some cases the man's relationship with, but not his care of, his children would be the subject of comment. Thus, while both men and women were presented to the court, whenever possible in the context of a family, the respective gender roles were very different. Men were expected to contribute to the upkeep of wife and children, and their efforts in doing so were to involve them in a conventional and non-criminal life of paid employment and family recreation. Women were expected to have a much closer involvement with the family household. This expectation was expressed by a magistrate:

> ... most women ... do have a degree of tie to the everyday care of their children in a way that a lot of men, otherwise responsible and sensible men, don't.

Where the woman had paid employment this would allow her to contribute financially to the household, but it would not detract from her responsibilities for the caring and nurturing of other family members. Expectations concerning the woman's involvement in the home were apparent in the probation officers' practices when making home visits to male and female defendants. To construct a report on a woman the probation officer would usually talk to the defendant in her home, and take note of her surroundings. Much was inferred from the way in which the woman had discharged her domestic duties. The woman's identity was revealed, it was assumed, by the material conditions of her home. The total involvement in the domestic role, which was expected of a woman, was also demonstrated by the probation officers' practice in making a home visit to a male defendant. When constructing a report on a man, the probation officer used the home visit to speak to the woman of the household, and incorporate her comments into the report. The 'caring' component of the woman's role is extended to include mediating with agents of the outside world who intrude into the home.

In this chapter I have argued that women are most vulnerable to the constraints and controls operating within family life. This may explain their low rate of representation in the criminal statistics. It may also explain the correlation, noted in recent research, between marital status and sentence for women but not for men (Nagel, 1981; Farrington and Morris, 1983), i.e. courts implicitly recognise the degree of control to which women are subject within the family. The work of Kruttschnitt (1982), discussed in Chapter 2, supports this argument.

Familial ideology, summary justice and cultural reproduction

The predominance of familial ideology in courtroom discourse is an acknowledgement of the role which the family plays in the socialisation and social control of members of society.

Sociologists from a range of perspectives have recognised that the family is the dominant means of socialisation into the mores of any society (Parsons and Bales, 1956; Marcuse, 1972; Young and Willmott, 1962; Fletcher, 1966; Sharpe, 1976). As a recent critique of the family argues:

> . . . the family remains a vigorous agency of class placement and an efficient mechanism for the creation and transmission of gender inequality. (Barrett and McIntosh, 1982:29)

It is in conjunction with the family that other social institutions operate as sites of cultural reproduction. One such institution is the legal system. Courts are responsible for the enforcement of the formal rules of society, and in carrying out this task they also enforce the informal, or unwritten, rules which regulate social relations between the classes and sexes.

As I have pointed out, the magistrates' courts deal with the majority of offenders in this country. Typically status differences within the court correspond to status differences beyond the court; that is to say middle-class magistrates deal with working class defendants. Chapter 6 discusses the Hillbury magistrates' reactions to this situation. In interview they expressed their awareness of the class differences between the defendants and the majority of the bench. They also expressed their concern that the defendants show a proper respect for the court. It is not sufficient that the process of law should take place, and exact retribution from the offender. The magistrates also demanded that the defendants should acquiesce in the process, and should reveal this acquiesence by their demeanour. In so doing the defendants acknowledge the authority of the magistrates, and the legitimacy of the social system from which such authority is derived. By such practices class relations are reinforced.

Gender relations are reinforced by continuous reference to the dominant model of the nuclear family as a bench mark of normality. As I have argued in Chapters 4 and 5, and earlier in this chapter, this is a model which is particularly oppressive of women.

The relevance of the present study is not confined to the court which was the focus of the fieldwork. The discussion of the equality of the defendants goes beyond the day-to-day practice at Hillbury; it is located at the level of ideological discourse. This discourse permeates not only the judicial process of Hillbury Court, but also the legal statutes and social policy which relate to the family (Brophy and Smart, 1985; Gittins, 1985). Prior to further research, there is no reason to believe that other courts would not employ this discourse in a similar manner. Furthermore, the issues raised in this study have relevance beyond the criminal justice system and the discourses of statute and policy. By focusing on the implications of the uncritical use of the dominant model of the family I have, I hope, alerted readers to the problems raised by the use of this model in other areas – at other sites of cultural reproduction, e.g. the education system, the labour market, the mass media.

Women and men, girls and boys are situated within the context of this model of the family in schools, i.e. in classrooms and staffrooms, in text books and reports. Michelle Stanworth (1985) asked a group of teachers to anticipate what pupils would be doing in five years' time. She found a tendency to discuss the boys in relation to jobs involving responsibility and authority, but to discuss girls in relation to marriage. Of one girl who was expected to go to university, and who was considering a career in law, a teacher said:

> Well, I can see her having a family, and having them jolly well organised. They'll get up at the right time and go to school at the right time, wearing the right clothes. Meals will be ready when her husband gets home. She'll handle it jolly well. (Stanworth, 1985:141–2)

Other work has demonstrated the home-centredness of women and girls in teachers' attitudes, text book images and educational policy (e.g. Buswell, 1981; Whyte, 1983; Wolpe, 1974).

In the work place, too, women and men are seen in the context of their expected relationship to the family, i.e. to a particular model of the family:

Organisations are said to be 'run like a family', the highest compliment that a man can receive is that he is a 'good family man' (women are never accrued the compliment of being a 'good family woman', as by definition they are assumed to be just that). (Gittins, 1985:155)

While men are seen in relation to their families, they are not expected to be primarily, almost exclusively, family-centred, in the way that women are.

Nothing illustrates the force of this doctrine better than the message, consistently reinforced in headlines, cartoons and jokes that the women at Greenham Common should not merely stop protesting, but that they should be *at home* carrying out their allotted, role-appropriate tasks in their proper place. (Heidensohn, 1985:188. Original emphasis.)

The mass media, from soap opera and advertisement to drama and documentary, consistently present women and men within the context of the ideologically dominant model of the family, and discuss them in relation to gender roles appropriate to this model. The courts are only one among many sites of the reproduction of the dominant ideology – and of the model of the family which is part of that ideology.

Conclusion

My research began with a question concerning the equality of men and women before the court. It concludes by recognising that within its own terms Hillbury Court treats men and women equally, i.e. they receive similar sentences when they appear in similar circumstances. However, men and women rarely appear in similar circumstances – the differences in their recorded criminal involvements are as marked as the differences between the sexes in other areas of life. Formal equality within the strictly defined area of the court does not affect the substantial inequality of women and men who appear before the court.

Men and women are located within different structural spheres. They are socialised, educated and employed to act and react in different ways. These differences are most forcefully expressed within the family. By supporting the dominant model of the family the court is contributing to the cultural reproduction of society and, thereby, to the continued subordination of women. The inequalities that women experience elsewhere in society are endorsed by the process of cultural reproduction operating within the court. An examination of the familial ideology that underlies summary justice reveals that women are not equal to men in court, since the court is operating from a perspective which defines women as different and subordinate. By endorsing the dominant model of the family, the court endorses the social relationships which are generated and reinforced by that model. It endorses the gender-roles which impel women and men into separate and unequal spheres. By judging both female and male defendants in the context of their families, the court displays not impartiality, or equality of treatment, but its role in preserving differences based on sexual inequality.

This role is played through the medium of the prevailing ideology, through the use of a world-view which is taken for granted by the courtroom participants. Spoken and written arguments are addressed to common-sense notions of reality. They rely on a shared and undisputed model of the social world and particularly of the family. The divisions and inequalities which form part of the model are not discussed in court. The model is so familiar that it is accepted as inevitable or 'natural'. Familial ideology is masked by familiar rhetoric.

To challenge the prevailing model of the family, and its concomitant gender roles, it would be necessary to pose the defendants' problems and their solution in terms other than those of their correspondence to or deviation from the nuclear family. It would be necessary to consider alternatives to the prevailing social arrangements and thereby to challenge the divisions of class and gender which characterise this society. But it is unlikely that the court, or any other state apparatus, could do this, since to do so would be to challenge the social structure of the system from which the court derives its authority.

Meanwhile women and men remain unequal in the magistrates' court as they are in any social situation which does not challenge the prevailing definitions of their respective places within the social system. The few women and men who appear in similar circumstances may receive similar sentences; however, this does not demonstrate equality when the processes determining such sentences, and the sentences of the majority of defendants, are rooted in an ideology which celebrates inequality.

Ultimately the predominance of familial ideology in the discourse of summary justice reveals the magistrates' court as yet another site of sexual inequality. Gender divisions, like class divisions, are endorsed by the judicial process and:

Justice is the means by which established injustices are sanctioned. (Anatole France, *Crainquebille* (1904))

Research appendix

The town

The research for the case study was carried out during 1980–1982, by observation, interview and document analysis, at a magistrates' court on the edge of London. For the purposes of this work the area is called Hillbury, and the court is Hillbury Magistrates' Court. Pseudonyms are used to protect the anonymity of the defendants and respondents.

The population of the borough of Hillbury at the time of the 1971 census was approximately 175,000 and 52 per cent were recorded as economically active. Of those in paid employment, 43 per cent worked within the borough. Many of the jobs in the borough are to be found in public administration, and financial and professional services. There is a low proportion of manufacturing jobs.

Hillbury is an especially busy shopping centre, drawing people from outside the town. Hillbury is also busy by night when it becomes a resort for people seeking entertainment in restaurants, wine bars, clubs and pubs. Since the town centre is small and densely populated this influx of visitors contributes to the traffic problems. A number of offences related to traffic, public order and shoplifting may be seen to arise partly from the characteristics of the area.

Burglary is a frequent crime in this borough, which has a high proportion of residents in the professional and managerial socio-economic groups. At the beginning of 1978 it was estimated that some 58 per cent of households were owner-occupied, 15 per cent were rented from the local authority, 2 per cent were rented from a housing association and 25 per cent were rented privately.

Hillbury is a prosperous borough with areas of expensive property, and amenities to cater for the owners. It also has a number of properties, owned by the local authority, which are notorious for the frequency with which the residents come before the court. The conspicuous consumption of the affluent overshadows, but does not completely hide, the poverty in parts of the area.

The court

Hillbury Magistrates' Court is a modern building and appears to be a pleasant place in which to work. On the ground floor are the fines office, the clerks' offices, the secretarial office, and the warrant office. The warrant officers are police officers with full-time court duties. Below the warrant office are the cells and a kitchen in which a matron cooks meals for the prisoners and the warrant officers. She also acts as chaperone to female prisoners.

There are five court rooms on the first floor of the building. Courts 1 and 2 are more formal in arrangement than Courts 3, 4 and 5. Crime cases from Hillbury are heard in Court 1, and in Court 2. Traffic offences, juvenile and domestic cases are heard in the other courts.

The week at Hillbury Court usually has the following pattern:

Monday:	a.m.	two crime courts, one traffic court
	p.m.	one traffic court (written guilty pleas)
Tuesday:	a.m.	two domestic courts
	p.m.	applications court (dealing with summonses, warrants)
Wednesday:	a.m.	two crime courts, two traffic courts
	p.m.	local authority prosecutions (e.g. food and drugs offences, car parks offences)
Thursday:	a.m.	two crime courts, one traffic court, one court set aside for special cases
	p.m.	that will take a long time and may run into the afternoon

Friday:	a.m.	two courts dealing with crime and traffic, two or three juvenile courts,
	p.m.	juvenile courts may continue into the afternoon

Other courts may sit as necessary.

The building is new and the acoustics are good, so many of the indignities suffered by defendants in other courts are not inflicted here (Carlen, 1976:21). Nevertheless, the divisions and hierarchies within the court are demonstrated and reinforced by the positions ascribed to different participants. The magistrates sit on a raised platform. The clerk, too, is raised, but not quite so high. Other participants are on the same level, but assigned to a particular position within the court.

Below is a plan of Court 1; Court 2 is a mirror image.

Hillbury Probation Office occupies part of the court building, but has its own entrance.

The probation service always has at least one officer on court duty, and there is usually an assistant officer in each of the two main courts. In addition an officer is usually present if a case arises involving either a social inquiry report that she/he has recently prepared, or involving a defendant already assigned to that probation officer.

The magistrates sit in groups of two or three. There are usually three, with at least one experienced magistrate. The rotas of magistrates constructed by the senior clerks are designed to give each individual magistrate a balanced experience of court work. All magistrates deal with crime and traffic offences, but only those who are members of the domestic panel and the juvenile panel sit in domestic and juvenile courts. Each magistrate should sit 26 times a year and I was told by the chief clerk that the Lord Chancellor's office disapproves of magistrates sitting too often. This means that those on the domestic and juvenile panels have less experience of traffic and crime courts, but nevertheless there is an attempt to keep their rotas balanced.

Journalists sit on the press bench; their presence was a source of much concern to the defendants who feared publicity.

Members of the public and waiting defendants sit in the public benches at the back of the court.

While the criminal courts in mainland Britain are public places, it was necessary to negotiate access to personnel and documents if the research was to move beyond observation from the public benches. I approached the Home Office and said that I was involved in research into the offences and sentences of women defendants in a magistrates' court. I asked for permission to consult the court registers and social inquiry reports, and to interview magistrates and probation officers. I was told that there would be no official objections to such work if there was no objection from Hillbury Court. In any matter relating to the magistrates' court, the clerk to the justices is a key figure. At Hillbury I was fortunate in finding that the clerk and the senior probation officer were both sympathetic to sociological research. Through them I gained access to areas which might have proved difficult or unattainable.

The fieldwork

Biography played an important part in the construction and execution of this research. Since 1976 I had been teaching an undergraduate course on the sociology of deviance and social control, and it was the paucity of empirical work on women in the British criminal justice system that led me to begin this work. In 1979 I registered as a part-time post-graduate student at the London School of Economics. As I was teaching full-time for most of the research period (1979–1983) the work is spread over a longer time than would otherwise be necessary.

From 1979 to 1980 I spent time in libraries and research seminars, familiarising myself with the relevant literature and aspects of methodology. During 1980 I spent two mornings a week and during 1981 one morning a week, observing courtroom interaction. During the summer vacations of 1980 and 1981, I examined the court registers and noted the recorded details on all cases heard during the period from which the observations came. This was done to establish whether the cases I had seen were representative of the cases before the court.

I was given sabbatical leave for the academic year 1981–1982 and so was able to work full-time on the research. This time I used to analyse social inquiry reports and to interview probation officers, magistrates, court clerks and police officers. The results of this work, and of the courtroom observations, were written up as a first draft of the final study. From 1982–83 this draft was revised, so that the final product could be presented in 1984 as a Ph.D. thesis (Eaton, M.E., 1984). This book is derived from the thesis but much material not immediately relevant to the main argument has been omitted. In this appendix I discuss only those aspects of the research which relate to the content of the book.

The court: observation and document analysis

I concentrated my observations in the crime courts, which were held in the more formal court rooms. Each morning a list of the day's cases is displayed in the foyer of the court, from this I could tell which court would have the greatest number of female defendants and I would carry out my observations in that court. Since women form such a small proportion of all defendants there were days when no women were appearing. However, I then chose a court by the cases which might provide comparative data (e.g. men on charges of shoplifting). Once I had selected a court all the cases were observed and noted.

During that time I saw a total of 321 complete cases, consisting of 210 cases involving male defendants and 111 cases involving female defendants. Eight of the men and eight of the women appeared in couples as co-defendants charged with the same offence. Three of these couples were legally represented, and so were 32 other men and 25 other women.

I also saw ten cases in which the legal representative made a plea that the defendant be granted bail while the case was remanded.

Other cases were remanded, but bail was readily granted, and there were cases that were begun or completed on days when I was not at court.

Since my study was initially concerned with those areas of judicial discretion which may be the site of differential or discriminatory treatment, I decided to focus on those cases in which the defendant is present in court to answer a charge (i.e. not motoring offences since many offenders plead guilty by letter). Even when the defendant is present much of the courtroom procedure follows a routine. It is only in exceptional circumstances that the routine is broken. In order to learn more about the practices of courtroom personnel it is necessary to examine the routine and usual, and to contrast such cases with those that are treated differently.

Each morning in court I made notes on the formal and informal proceedings, and when the magistrates retired to consider a case I talked to different members of the court in order to learn something of their attitudes and opinions. The notes were written up shortly afterwards, when I had left the court.

During the summer vacations of 1980 and 1981, I examined the court registers and noted the details recorded on all the cases heard during 1980. From the registers I learned the name, sex, age, address and brief details of the charges brought against each defendant. The place of trial, plea and outcome, including requests for reports, were noted. The court registers were used to discover, firstly, which crimes showed the highest concentration of female offenders, and, secondly, what were the most usual sentences for those crimes.

During 1980 the crimes (excluding summary motoring) which involved more than five per cent of the female defendants appearing at Hillbury court were as follows:

Shoplifting	132	32%
Other theft	28	7%
Deception	27	7%
Drug offences	20	5%
Drunkenness	48	12%
TV Licence (non-payment)	26	6%
B.R. fare (non-payment)	22	5%

Only in these cases did female defendants appear in sufficient numbers to make a comparison with male defendants feasible. Even here, however, the circumstances of any particular offence, and the past history and current background of the offender, make it extremely difficult to match like with like in order to compare the male and female defendants charged with the same offence.

Some readers may be surprised that I do not include offences related to prostitution. I can only say that during my time at Hillbury only two women were charged with soliciting. Perhaps the location does not offer sufficient anonymity.

I selected four areas in order to explore the treatment of men and women before the court. They were selected on the basis of factors noted in courtroom observation, and the relatively high number of women involved. Three areas concern offences, and the other concerns public pleas on behalf of defendants. The areas are as follows:

1 Drunk (and disorderly)

These offences were chosen as an example of cases characterised chiefly by the routine way in which they were disposed of. The size of fine was usually predictable. Social inquiry reports on such defendants were extremely rare.

The court registers recorded a high proportion of defendants involved in these offences: 20 per cent of the men and 12 per cent of the women appearing at Hillbury in 1980 did so on such charges.

A sample of 74 cases (58 men and 16 women) was observed. Most of these received routine fines.

2 Drug Offences

This category was chosen because it contained some cases that are usually dealt with in a routine manner, and others that were deemed to merit other disposals.

The court registers revealed that 87 men and 17 women had been convicted on drug related charges, and that in the majority of cases (79 per cent) the defendant had received a fine of £25 or £30.

A sample of 27 cases (20 men and 7 women) was observed. Most of these received routine fines.

3 Shoplifting

This offence gives the best opportunity for comparing male and female defendants, since it is here that numbers most closely correspond.

The court registers revealed that 222 men and 122 women appeared at Hillbury, in 1980, on charges of shoplifting. Of these defendants 25 of the men (11 per cent) and 33 of the women (27 per cent) were the subject of a social inquiry report. A higher proportion of the women (27 per cent) than of the men (7 per cent) received the more lenient sentences of a conditional discharge or probation.

A sample of 79 cases (28 men and 51 women) was observed. In the sample, 49 per cent of the women and 18 per cent of the men received the comparatively lighter sentences of conditional discharge or probation. Of these defendants 59 per cent of the women and 25 per cent of the men were first-time offenders.

The court registers reveal a defendant's name, sex, age, and address. They record brief details of the offence and the sentence. From sitting in court an observer may learn more about the circumstances of the offence, and the defendant's background, as well as the way in which the case was conducted. For each of the three offences examined – drunkenness, drug abuse and shoplifting – the court registers reveal the patterns of crime and punishment as they relate to men and women at Hillbury. The samples of cases observed in these three areas were then used to discuss usual and unusual treatment of men and women in relation to the gravity of the offence, the circumstances of the offender, and the previous convictions. In this way it was possible to decide whether the women before the court were treated differently from the men because of their sex, or because of their circumstances.

4 Pleas of Mitigation

In the cases observed, 35 of the male defendants and 28 of the female defendants were legally represented. Pleas of mitigation were offered on behalf of all but one man. The arguments used in these pleas were noted and categorised in order to discover, firstly, whether different arguments were used for men and women, and, secondly, what such arguments revealed about the consensus on which courtroom interaction is based.

Findings from the observations

The majority of cases were dealt with in a routine manner with little attention paid to the circumstances of an individual offender. Defendants of either sex who were charged with drunkenness appeared as the first business of the day. They usually pleaded guilty, were unrepresented, and were dispatched with a fine of £10 for being drunk and £15 to £40, depending on the extent of the alleged disorderliness, for being drunk and disorderly. The exceptions to this routine were rare and involved very unusual circumstances not related to the sex of the defendant. Minor drug offences were also the subject of routine treatment. Most men and women were fined £25 or £30 for a first offence of possessing cannabis.

A fine can be seen as a simple way of punishing an offender. If the magistrates decide this is inappropriate, they have access to a wide range of alternatives at their disposal. However, before using one of these alternatives they would usually request a social inquiry report. During the period of observation, the only sentences given without a report were fines and conditional discharges. And conditional discharges were usually given only after a plea of mitigation had been made by a lawyer.

Non-routine matters were characterised by the intervention of a lawyer or a probation officer. In most cases a lawyer, familiar with the court, judicial attitudes and sentencing policies, was able to present the defendant to the magistrate as someone deserving of a lenient rather than a severe sentence. Most lawyers spend much of their time trying to convince the magistrate that the case is a non-routine matter, and the client (male or female) is not a 'real criminal'. By stressing the financial and personal circumstances of the defendant, a lawyer may persuade the magistrates to decide that help rather than punishment is appropriate. In some cases such pleas of mitigation resulted in a conditional discharge, in others in a request for a social inquiry report. An analysis of the pleas of mitigation showed that for men and women the family is used to explain or excuse the offence. (This was discussed in Chapter 4.)

In requesting a social inquiry report magistrates invite a contribution from a probation officer. A higher proportion of women were the subject of such reports, and this can be seen as leading to the situation noted both at Hillbury and nationally in which the proportion of women who become the subject of probation orders is much higher than the proportion of men who do. However, when the reasons behind a request for a report are considered, the matter becomes one in which, once again, the circumstances rather than the sex of the defendant are the relevant factor.

Social inquiry reports were requested when the magistrates were considering custody. Few women had either the record of previous convictions or the involvement in serious crime to merit imprisonment. Other reasons for requesting a social inquiry report concerned the non-routine nature of the case, specifically the indication of 'social problems' in the background. Adults who begin offending after the age of 21 were likely to become the subject of a social inquiry report on their second or third appearance. Magistrates expressed the belief that some unknown factor, or social problem, must be causing this new pattern of behaviour. The presence of children, particularly in the case of a single parent, was also likely to give rise to a request for a report. Both factors would influence the magistrates irrespective of the sex of the defendant, however both factors are more likely to occur with women rather than men. Women over 21 are twice as likely as men to have no previous convictions when they appear in court (Home Office 1979) and only 1 in 10 single parents is a lone father (Study Commission on the Family, 1981).

During the fieldwork I found no difference in the request for medical reports on women and men defendants.

While I was coming to the conclusion that the few men and women who appear in similar circumstances receive similar treatment, I was also becoming aware that the use of language within the court has implications for the reproduction of gender divisions. In order to explore this aspect of courtroom activity, I decided to focus on the pleas of mitigation made in court, the social inquiry reports prepared by probation officers and the perspectives and responses of magistrates. Observation in court gave me access to the pleas of mitigation; however, to take the research further it was necessary for me to obtain access to social inquiry reports and to learn something about their construction. I also wanted to talk to magistrates, as the ultimate decision makers, about their role in the process of summary justice.

Probation Officers: Document Analaysis and Interviews

In the cases observed, social inquiry reports were requested on 37 of the men and 35 of the women. There is evidence of a positive association between the recommendations made by probation officers in such reports, and the magistrates' decisions (Thorpe and Pease, 1976). Analysis of these reports was essential to any understanding of the processes at work in the judicial treatment of men and women. Since these documents are confidential, I applied to the chief probation officer of the district for permission to look at the social inquiry reports and, also, to interview the Hillbury probation officers. My request was supported by the senior probation officer at Hillbury, to whom I had been introduced by the chief clerk. I was given permission to proceed with the research.

In order to compare two groups of adults, to whom similar arguments might be expected to apply, the sample was confined to reports on people over 21. Although those over 17 appear before the adult court, I decided not to include these as the arguments presented in these cases are often similar to those used for juveniles. Exceptions were made where a co-defendant under 21 appeared with someone over 21. A content analysis was then carried out on each report. The different sections on childhood, current background, health, the offence and the probation officer's recommendations were examined to discover whether there was a difference in the way these sections were constructed for men and women defendants.

During my time in the courtroom I had many opportunities to speak to the probation officers. However, in order to learn more of the attitudes and opinions which could be expected to influence their practice, I wanted to spend some time in uninterrupted discussion with each officer. I decided that a loosely structured interview would be the best way of focusing on specific aspects of the probation officer's life and work. Being loosely structured such an interview would allow the probation officer to contribute material which would not be elicited by a tightly structured questionnaire which had pre-defined the relevant matters.

Table A.1 Probation officers interviewed

Sex	Status	Years as P.O.	Former occupations
M	Snr. P.O.	30	–
F	Snr. P.O.	12	Teacher
M	P.O.	10	Army
F	P.O.	10	Interior design; manageress of a shop
F	P.O.	8	Secretary
F	P.O.	5	Charity organiser
F	P.O.	4	Dancer
F	P.O.	2 + 1	Child-care
M	P.O.	2	Teacher; work on a drug project
M	P.O.	2	Teacher

The interviews lasted between 30 minutes and 2 hours depending on the degree of discussions elicited by the topics raised.

Discussion centred on four main topics:

i) the professional biography of the respondent;
ii) the current work of the respondent;
iii) observations on the requesting and preparation of social inquiry reports;
iv) women as defendants and clients.

Each qualified probation officer, i.e. those who write the social inquiry reports, was interviewed.

The sample consisted of men and women with a range of experience. The majority had worked in other areas before coming to probation work.

The analysis of the social inquiry reports revealed an implicit model of the family, and the relationship of men and women within that model. The probation officers' ideas concerning their practice have been incorporated into a discussion of the processes by which that model is revealed and reinforced. This material was prevented and analysed in Chapter 5.

Magistrates: Observation and Interview

In 1982 there were 49 men and 44 women acting as Justices of the Peace at Hillbury court. The 'chairman' was male and there were six male and two female 'deputy chairmen' ('chairmen' is a members' term, it refers to a senior magistrate either within the local bench, or sitting in a particular court). A further 24 men and 14 women constituted the 'assistant chairmen'.

During my two years in court I had seen various combinations of justices at their judicial tasks, and I had had ample opportunity of observing their public reactions to and comments on the cases before them. I wanted to talk to a group of these magistrates to learn, from them as individuals, their attitudes towards the female defendants who came before them.

A number of issues were selected for discussion in a loosely structured interview. These issues included:

i) the individual magistrate's position as a member of the local community and the relevance of personal experience to judicial practice;
ii) typical female offenders, unusal female offenders and the concept of 'normal' female crime;
iii) the putative causes of crime;
iv) factors influencing judgment and sentencing;
v) and the professional involvement of police, probation officers and lawyers.

The focus of the interview was the magistrate's attitude to the female offender, but this was set in the wider context of the magistrate's experience of all defendants before the court, and the magistrate's attitude to the role of women within the community.

The chief clerk arranged for me to meet a large number of J.P.s, and explain my research to them. He invited me to be the guest speaker at a meeting of the magistrates. Once they had completed their business of welcoming new members to the bench, being advised of changes in the law and sentencing practice, and deciding on a venue for the annual dinner, I addressed them for 25 minutes on my research on female offenders.

I described the picture of female offending that emerges from the official statistics and told them that I was trying to understand this more fully by means of a case study based on their court, and so would like to interview some of the magistrates. I was able to develop some points in more detail as I joined the magistrates later for a glass of wine in the retiring room.

On the day following that meeting I met the chief clerk, to select possible interviewees. Two of the J.P.s preset the previous evening had expressed a hostility to the social sciences and had told the chief clerk that they did not wish to be interviewed. Ten of the J.P.s had only just been appointed, and 46 were not present at the meeting. This left a possible 35 J.P.s who were aware of the nature of my work, had some experience on the bench, and had not expressed any definite refusal to be interviewed.

I decided to telephone these 35 J.P.s and arrange interviews wherever possible. Some were away on holiday or business, and one expressed a reluctance as he was very busy. The reactions of the others varied from enthusiasm to wary agreement.

Eventually I had a sample of 30. A brief description of each member is contained in Table A.2. There were 17 men and 13 women, which is approximately one third of the bench. The majority of these were middle-class with professional or business occupations, or a life-style that allowed the magistrate to work voluntarily for the community. One male member of the sample, the engineer, could be considered to be working class. Most of the magistrates were involved in local community or charity work and/or local politics. The engineer was an active trade unionist. Occupations have been classified according to the Registrar General's Social Class Scale.

The occupations of the female magistrates shown in Table A.2 are those given by the respondents. A majority described themselves as housewives, two added that they had part-time paid employment, and one considered her voluntary work to be her full-time occupation and housekeeping her part-time work. In assessing the social class of these women, I decided to classify them according to their husband's occupation. By so doing I am not suggesting that they enjoyed the autonomy and resources of their salaried husbands. However, they enjoyed a greater degree of control over their lives than that experienced by the female defendants, many of whom were also described as housewives. The Registrar General's scale is a blunt instrument by which to gauge the variations in allegiances, resources and autonomy of a group of individuals; in this case it serves to show the differences in the social position of the judging and the judged.

Whenever I phoned a prospective interviewee, I would remind the magistrates of the talk I had given and ask if he or she were willing to take part in the research by being interviewed for approximately 20 to 30 minutes. I suggested either the court, or their home, as a suitable venue. The court was by no means as satisfactory a venue as the magistrate's home since it meant finding a day when that J.P. was next at Hillbury and if an early interview was not feasible it meant waiting for the court to rise at any time from 11.30 a.m. to 2.00 p.m. The staff of the court made an office

Table A.2 Magistrates interviewed

Sex of JP	Status of JP	Length of Service (years)	Full-time Occupation	Part-time Occupation	Social Class*	Voluntary Community Work	Voluntary Church-based Work	Local Political Work	Trade Union Work
M	Deputy	29	Retired computer consultant		II			x	
M	Deputy	26	Retired architect		I			x	
M	Deputy	25	Retired accountant		I	x			
F	Deputy	21	Housewife		II	x		x	
M	Asst	19	Architect		I		x		
M	Asst	18	Customs & excise		II	x			
M	Asst	16	Manufacturer		II	x			
M	Asst	16	Bank manager		II	x			
M	Asst	12	Minister of religion		I				
M	Asst	12	Restaurateur		IIIN	x			
M	Asst	10	Head teacher		II				
M	Asst	7	Surveyor		I	x			
M	Asst	6	Head teacher		II	x		x	
M	Asst	5	Senior executive		II	x		x	

Sex		No.	Occupation		Social class*				
F	Asst	24	Retired charity worker		I		x	x	x
F	Asst	18	Voluntary church work	Housewife	I		x		x
F	Asst	14	Housewife		II		x x		x
F	Asst	14	Housewife		I		x		
F	Asst	7	Senior civil servant		II				
F	Asst	6	Speech therapist		I		x		
M	Asst	6	H.E. lecturer		II		x	x	
M	Asst	4	Computer consultant		II				
M	Asst	4	Head teacher		II		x		x
M	Asst	3	Foreman engineer		IIIM				x
F	Asst	14	Housewife		II		x x		
F	Asst	6	Housewife		I				
F	Asst	5	Housewife	School nurse	II			x	
F	Asst	5	Interior decorator		I				
F	Asst	4	Housewife	Secretary	I		x		x
F	Asst	1	Housewife		I		x		

*Registrar General's Social Class Classification

available to me but it did not have the relaxed atmosphere of a home, and the whole interaction was more formal and closely focused on the matter in hand. Most of the women invited me to their home for the interview. Most of the men suggested the court, and some suggested their places of work. Where the interview took place in the home there was usually some general conversation over a cup of coffee or tea and I was able to learn far more about the life-style and general opinions of the magistrate in question. Since there was a local election taking place at this time political party posters in the windows gave an indication of political allegiances.

Table A.3 Place of interview for the sample of magistrates

| Magistrates | | Place of interview | |
	Court	Home	Work-place
Female 13	3	10	–
Male 17	9	4	4

Most of the magistrates had no objection to being tape-recorded. Some required an assurance about the use to which the tapes would be put. Some were a little reluctant at first but eventually agreed. I always asked if I might tape and gave the reason that writing in long hand would take considerably more time. Two women refused to be taped, and these were by far the most nervous of respondents, so much so that I can only be grateful that they actually consented to be interviewed since the whole venture seemed rather an ordeal for them. In many cases the actual interview lasted for longer than 30 minutes, and some of the home visits lasted for up to two hours.

Two themes not anticipated in the schedule arose during the course of the interview: the magistrates' attitudes to the defendant's social class, and the magistrates' consciousness of their own authority.

The material from the interviews was used in Chapter 6 to examine the implications of the attitudes and opinions expressed by the magistrates, as they relate to defendants, the local community, and the working of the court.

The material gathered from interviews, observation and document analysis was examined and discussed in the context of existing work on the judicial process (especially that of Carlen 1976 and McBarnet 1981) and of work on the position of women in contemporary British society. What goes on in courts can be fully understood only within the wider context of the society of which the criminal justice system is a part. In presenting the results of the fieldwork, I have attempted to show how the specific instances examined tell us more about the subjugation of women throughout society. By becoming aware of the routine reproduction of subordination in one area we can become alert to the existence of similar processes in other areas. With a greater sensitivity to the pervasiveness of the processes of sexism, we are in a stronger position to challenge them.

Notes

Chapter One: Justice, crime and social control

1 Of course one might ask how much they allow an accurate representation of the lives of most men. The distortion that pre-existing categories may cause in any account of any social reality is a subject much debated by phenomenologists and ethnomethodologists. (Filmer *et al.*, 1971). Furthermore, much valuable work has come from the Birmingham Centre for Contemporary Cultural Studies which, under the label 'cultural studies', has moved across the boundaries that exist in traditional sociology (Hall and Jefferson, 1976; Hall *et al.*, 1980).
2 King and May (1985) have recently published the results of a survey into the representation of Black people on the bench.

Chapter Three: The magistrates' court

1 The relatively high proportion of women is due to my practice of selecting the courtroom with the largest number of female defendants. The proportion of female defendants at Hillbury was the same as the national average, approximately 12 per cent.
2 I did not find a repetition of the pattern observed by Pearson in her study of magistrates' courts in Cardiff (Pearson, 1976:267). She found that women were

treated leniently, compared to men on similar charges, when they appeared either alone or as co-defendants.

Chapter Four: Pleas of mitigation

1 The material in this chapter originally appeared in Eaton, 1983.
2 The attitude expressed by some members of the Criminal Law Revision Committee shows their reluctance to see official intervention on this matter, and their disapproval of wives who would seek redress in law:

> The type of questions which investigating police officers would have to ask would be greatly resented by husbands and families. The family ties would be severed and the wife with children would have to cope with her emotional, social and financial problems as best she could; and *possibly the children might resent what she had done to their father.* (Criminal Law Revision Committee 1980, Para. 33, emphasis added.)

I am grateful to Carol Smart for drawing my attention to this passage.

Chapter Five: Social inquiry reports

1 See the Research Appendix in this volume, for details concerning access to these documents.
2 Although Section 2 of the Domestic Proceedings and Magistrates' Courts Act, 1978, allows a partner to apply for a maintenance order while the couple is cohabiting, Section 25 states that:

> . . . the order shall cease to have effect if after that date the parties continue to live with each other, or resume living with each other, for a continuous period exceeding six months. *(Statutes in Force: Domestic Proceedings and Magistrates' Courts Act 1978*, London: HMSO, p. 27)

Chapter Six: Magistrates' talk

1 Each year the Lord Chancellor is supplied with details of the age, sex, occupation and politics of each member of the bench. In order to maintain, or achieve, a degree of representation of the local community, the Lord Chancellor may recommend that new appointments fall into specific categories, currently under-represented. Magistrates must live or work within 15 miles of the division in which they sit. For further details see Burney (1979) and Skyrme (1979).
2 Magistrates are chosen from those who apply, by the local advisory committee of each bench. The membership of these committees is secret, supposedly to prevent lobbying. In many areas the committee consists of a group of local magistrates. Reasons for rejecting applicants are not given. While anyone may apply to become a

magistrate, most successful candidates are drawn from areas of political or community activity that have supplied existing magistrates (Burney, 1979).

3 In Inner London the names of those on the advisory committee are published.

4 These magistrates seemed unaware of the recommendation in Home Office Circular 59/1971, Para. 13, that probation officers should be free to express their opinions concerning sentence.

5 Social inquiry reports for Hillbury Court are always based on at least one interview of approximately one hour, and usually on a further interview, or a home visit. Other resources may also be used (see Chapter 5).

6 Probation officers preparing reports for Hillbury court are unable to 'aim' the report at a specific magistrate since the system of rotation does not allow them to predict who will be sitting when the case continues. This was not the case with the benches studied by Carlen (1976) and Burney (1979).

7 Magistrates receive a basic training which consists of lectures, visits to courts, prisons and borstals, and exercises in sentencing. This is essentially a practical training and rarely amounts to more than a total of 40 hours. Subsequent in-service courses are available for those who wish to avail themselves of these.

8 A London police constable receives an initial training of 16 weeks, followed by two years' probation.

9 Probation officers receive a two year professional training, or a one year professional training subsequent to university graduation.

10 Solicitors must successfully complete either:
    i) a law degree, followed by a one year professional course, followed by two years as an articled clerk in a solicitor's office,
    or
    ii) a non-law degree, followed by a two year professional course, followed by two years as an articled clerk.

11 Barristers must successfully complete either:
    i) a law degree, followed by a one year professional course, followed by a year's pupillage,
    or
    ii) a non-law degree, followed by a two year professional course, followed by a year's pupillage.

Chapter Seven: Summary justice and familial ideology

1 Anne Oakley's research revealed that women with young children worked an average of 77 hours a week; nearly twice as long as an industrial working week of 40 hours (Oakley, 1974:33).

2 The popularity of the sentimental ballad *No Charge* indicates the prevalence of this idea. The song, which itemises the many tasks performed by a mother for her child, was in the top twenty for six weeks in the early summer of 1976. (It was written by Harlen Howard, and recorded by J. J. Barrie on the Chopper Label by E.M.I. Music Publishing Co.) It is discussed further by Steedman (1982:127).

3 When, during the 1939–45 War, large numbers of women were needed in full-time paid employment outside the home, the state made provision for nurseries and canteens (Wilson, 1977:135).

Bibliography

ADLER, Freda (1975), *Sisters in Crime*, New York: McGraw-Hill.

ADLER, Freda and SIMON, Rita James, eds (1979), *The Criminology of Deviant Women*, Boston: Houghton Mifflin.

ALTHUSSER, Louis (1971), *Lenin and Philosophy and Other Essays*, London: New Left Books.

AMOS, Valerie and PARMAR, Pratibha (1984), 'Challenging Imperial Feminism', *Feminist Review* No. 17.

BALDWIN, John (1976), 'The Social Composition of the Magistracy', *British Journal of Criminology*, Vol. 16, pp. 171–4.

BARKER, Diana Leonard and ALLEN, Sheila, eds (1976), *Dependance and Exploitation in Work and Marriage*, London: Longman.

BARRETT, Michele and ROBERTS, Helen (1978), 'Doctors and their patients: The social control of women in general practice', in Smart and Smart (eds) op.cit.

BARRETT, Michele and MCINTOSH, Mary (1982), *The Anti-social Family*, London: Verso/NLB.

BARRTT, Michele and MCINTOSH, Mary (1985), 'Ethnocentrism and socialist-feminist theory', *Feminist Review* No. 20.

BARTLETT, David and WALKER, John (1973), *New Society*, 19th April.

BELL, Colin and NEWBY, Howard (1976), 'Husbands and wives: the dynamics of the deferential dialectic' in Barker and Allen (eds) op.cit.

BERNSTEIN, Basil (1971), *Class, Codes and Control*, London: Routledge and Kegan Paul.

BOWKER, Lee H. (1978), *Women, Crime, and the Criminal Justice System*, Lexington, Mass: D. C. Heath and Company.

BOX, Steven (1971), *Deviance, Reality and Society*, London: Holt, Rinehart and Winston.

BOX, Steven and HALE, Chris (1983), 'Liberation and Female Criminality in England and Wales' in *British Journal of Criminology*, vol. 23, no. 1, pp. 35–49.

BROPHY, Julia (1986), *Law, State and the Family: The Politics of Child Custody*, Unpublished Ph.D. thesis, Sheffield University.

BROPHY, Julia and SMART, Carol, (1981), 'From disregard to disrepute: the position of women in family law', *Feminist Review*, No. 9, pp. 3–16.

BROPHY, Julia and SMART, Carol, eds (1985), *Women-In-Law*, London: Routledge and Kegan Paul.

BROWN, G., BHROLCHAIN, M. N. and HARRIS, T. (1975), 'Social class and psychiatric disturbance among women in an urban population' *Sociology*, vol. 9, no. 2, May.

BRUNSDEN, Charlotte (1978), 'It is well known that by nature women are inclined to be rather personal', in Women's Studies Group Centre for Contemporary Cultural Studies, op.cit.

BURMAN, Sandra, ed. (1979), *Fit Work for Women* London: Croom Helm.

BURNEY, Elizabeth (1979), *J.P: Magistrate, Court and Community*, London: Hutchinson.

BUSWELL, C. (1981), 'Sexism in school routine and classroom practices', *Durham and Newcastle Review*, vol. 9, no. 46, pp. 195–200.

CAMPBELL, Ann (1981), *Girl Deliquents*, Oxford: Basil Blackwell.

CARLEN, Pat (1976), *Magistrates' Justice*, Oxford: Martin Robertson.

CARLEN, Pat (1983), *Women's Imprisonment*, London: Routledge and Kegan Paul.

CHESNEY-LIND, Meda (1973), 'Judicial enforcement of the female sex role: the family court and the female delinquent', *Issues in Criminology*, Fall, 1973, vol. 8, no. 2, pp. 51–69.

CHESNEY-LIND, Meda (1978), 'Chivalry re-examined: Women and the criminal justice system', in Bowker (ed.), op.cit.

CRIMINAL LAW REVISION COMMITTEE (1980), *Working Papers on Sexual Offences*, London: H.M.S.O.

CROSS, Rupert (1979), *Evidence*, London: Butterworth.

DAHL, Tove Stang and SNARE, Annika (1978), 'The coercion of privacy: A feminist perspective', in Smart and Smart (eds), op.cit.

DATESMAN, Susan, K. and SCARPITTI, Frank R., eds (1980), *Women, Crime and Justice*, New York: Oxford University Press.

DELL, Susanne (1971), *Silent in Court*, London: G. Bell & Sons.

DOBASH, R. and DOBASH, R. (1980), *Violence Against Wives* London: Open Books.

DONZELOT, Jaques (1979), *The Policing of Families*, London: Hutchinson.

DOUGLAS, Mary (1970), *Natural Symbols*, London: Barrie and Rockcliffe.

EATON, Mary (1983), 'Mitigating circumstances: Familiar rhetoric', *International Journal of the Sociology of Law*, vol. 11, pp. 385–400.

EATON, Mary (1984), *Familial ideology and summary justice: Gender divisions in a magistrates' court*, Unpublished Ph.D. thesis, London University.

EDWARDS, Susan, ed. (1985), *Gender, Sex and the Law*, London: Croom Helm.

EVERS, Helen (1981), 'Care or Custody? The Experience of Women Patients in Long-stay Geriatric Wards', in Hutter and Williams (eds), op.cit.

FARRINGTON, David and MORRIS, Allison (1983), 'Sex, Sentencing and Reconviction', *British Journal of Criminology*, vol. 23, no. 3, pp. 229–248.

FLETCHER, Ronald (1966), *The Family and Marriage in Britain*, Harmondsworth: Penguin.

FLUDE, Michael and AHIER, John, eds (1976), *Educability, Schools and Ideology*, London: Croom Helm.

FILMER, Paul, PHILLIPSON, Michael, SILVERMAN, David and WALSH, David (1972), *New Direction in Sociological Theory*, London: Collier Macmillan.

FINCH, Janet (1982), *Married to the Job*, London: Allen and Unwin.

GAVRON, Hannah (1966), *The Captive Wife*, London: Routledge and Kegan Paul.

GELSTHORPE, Lorraine (1984), *Exploring accounts of female offenders and their treatment in theory, policy and practice: Misconception and exaggeration*, Unpublished Ph.D. thesis, Cambridge University.

GIBBENS, T.C.N. and PRINCE, Joyce (1962), *Shoplifting*, London: Institute for the Study and Treatment of Delinquency.

GITTINS, Diana (1985), *The Family In Question: Changing Households & Familiar Ideologies*, London: Macmillan.

GREEN, Edward (1961), *Judicial Attitudes in Sentencing*, London: Macmillan.

GRIFFITH, J.A.G. (1977), *The Politics of the Judiciary*, Glasgow: Fontana.

HALL, Stuart and JEFFERSON, Tony, eds (1976), *Resistance through Rituals: Youth subcultures in post-war Britain*, London: Hutchinson.

HALL, Stuart, HOBSON, Dorothy, LOWE, Andrew and WILLIS, Paul (1980), *Culture, Media, Language*, London: Hutchinson.

HEIDENSOHN, Frances (1968), 'The deviance of women: a critique and an inquiry', *British Journal of Sociology*, vol. XIX, no. 2, pp. 160–175.

HEIDENSOHN, Frances (1985), *Women and Crime*, London: Macmillan.

HOBSON, Dorothy (1978), 'Housewives: isolation as oppression', in Women's Studies Group Centre for Contemporary Cultural Studies, op.cit.

HOME OFFICE, (1979), *Criminal Statistics, England and Wales, 1978*, London: H.M.S.O.

HOME OFFICE (1984), *Criminal Statistics, England and Wales, 1983*, London: H.M.S.O.

HOME OFFICE (1985), *Criminal Statistics, England and Wales, 1984*, London: H.M.S.O.

HUTTER, Bridget and WILLIAMS, Gillian, eds (1981), *Controlling Women: The Normal and The Deviant*, London: Croom Helm.

KAHN, Peggy (1985), 'Unequal Opportunities: Women, Unemployment and the Law', in Edwards (ed.), op.cit.

KING, Michael and MAY, Colin (1985), *Black Magistrates*, London: The Cobden Trust.

KLEIN, Doris (1973), 'The etiology of female crime: a review of the literature', *Issues in Criminology*, vol. 8, no. 2, pp. 3–30.

KRUTTSCHNITT, Candace (1982), 'Women, Crime and Dependency', *Criminology*, vol. 9, No. 4, pp. 495–513.

LAND, Hilary (1978), 'Who cares for the family?', *Journal of Social Policy*, No. 7, pp. 257–284.

LAND, Hilary (1980), 'The Family Wage', *Feminist Review*, No. 6, pp. 55–77.

LASCH, Christopher (1977), *Haven in a Heartless World*, New York: Basic Books.

MARCUSE, Herbert (1972), *Eros and Civilisation*, London: Abacus.

MCBARNET, Doreen (1981), *Conviction*, London: Macmillan.

MCANN, Kathryn (1985), 'Battered women and the law: the limits of the legislation', in Brophy and Smart (eds), op.cit.

MCINTOSH, Mary (1978), 'Who Needs Prostitutes? The ideology of male sexual needs' in Smart and Smart (eds), op.cit.

MCINTOSH, Mary (1979), 'The welfare state and the needs of the dependent family', in Burman, S. (ed.), op.cit.

MCLEOD, Eileen (1981), 'Man-made laws for men? The Street Prostitutes' Campaign Against Control' in Hutter and Williams (eds), op.cit.

MCLEOD, Eileen (1982), *Women Working: Prostitution Now*, London: Croom Helm.

MCROBBIE, Angela (1978), 'Working-class girls and the culture of femininity', in Women's Studies Group Centre for Contemporary Cultural Studies, op.cit.

MORRIS, Allison, ed. (1981), *Women and Crime*, University of Cambridge: Institute of Criminology.

MOULDS, Elizabeth (1980), 'Chivalry and paternalism: Disparities of treatment in the Criminal Justice System', in Datesman and Scarpitti (eds), op.cit.

NAGEL, Ilene (1981), 'Sex differences in the processing of criminal defendants', in Allison Morris (ed.), op.cit.

NAGEL, S. S. and WEITZMAN, L. J. (1971), 'Women as litigants', *The Hastings Law Journal*, vol. 23, no. 1, pp. 171–98.

OAKLEY, Ann (1974), *The Sociology of Housework*, London: Martin Robertson.

OAKLEY, Ann (1981), 'Normal motherhood: An exercise in self-control?' in Hutter and Williams (eds), op.cit.

O'DONOVAN, Katherine (1979), 'The male appendage – legal definitions of women', in Burman (ed.), op.cit.

OTTO, Shirley (1981), 'Women, alcohol and social control', in Hutter and Williams (eds), op.cit.

PAHL, Jan (1980), 'Patterns of money management within marriage', *Journal of Social Policy*, vol. 9, part 3.

PARSONS, Talcott and BALES, R. F. (1956), *Family: Socialization and Interaction Process*, London: Routledge and Kegan Paul.

PHILLIPSON, Chris (1981), 'Women in later life: patterns of control and subordination', in Hutter and Williams (eds), op.cit.

PEARSON, R. (1976), 'Women defendants in magistrates' courts', *British Journal of Law and Society*, vol. 3, no. 2, pp. 265–273.

POLLAK, Otto (1950), *The Criminality of Women*, Philadelphia: University of Pennsylvania Press.

POPE, Carl E. (1975), *Sentencing of California Felony Offenders*, Washington D.C.: Criminal Justice Research Centre.

POSTER, Mark (1978), *Critical Theory and the Family*, London: Pluto Press.

PROCEK, Eva (1981), 'Psychiatry and the Social Control of Women', in Morris (ed.), op.cit.

ROTTMAN, D. B. and SIMON, R. J. (1975), 'Women in the Court', *Chitty's Law Journal*, vol. 23, no. 52.

ROWETT, Colin and VAUGHAN, Phillip J. (1981), 'Women and Broadmoor: Treatment and control in a special hospital', in Hutter and Williams (eds), op.cit.

SACHS, A. and WILSON, J. H. eds (1978), *Sexism and The Law*, Oxford: Martin Robertson.

SAPIR, Edward (1949), *Culture, Language and Personality: Selected Essays*, D. Mandelbaum (ed.), California: University of California Press.

SHACKLADY-SMITH, Lesley (1978), 'Sexist Assumptions and Female Delinquency', in Smart and Smart (eds), op.cit.

SHARPE, Sue (1976), *Just Like a Girl*, Harmondsworth: Penguin.

SIMON, Rita James (1977), *Women and Crime*, Lexington, Mass: D.C. Heath and Co.

SKYRME, Thomas (1979), *The Changing Image of The Magistracy*, London: Macmillan.

SMART, Carol (1976), *Women, Crime and Criminology*, London: Routledge and Kegan Paul.

SMART, Carol (1981), 'Law and the control of women's sexuality: The case of the 1950s', in Hutter and Williams (eds), op.cit.

SMART, Carol (1984), *The Ties That Bind: Law in marriage and the reproduction of patriarchal relations*, London: Routledge and Kegan Paul.

SMART, Carol and SMART, Barry, eds (1978), *Women, Sexuality and Social Control*, London: Routledge and Kegan Paul.

STANWORTH, Michelle (1985), 'Just Three Quiet Girls', in Ungerson (ed.), op.cit.

STEDMAN JONES, Gareth (1971), *Outcast London*, Oxford: Oxford University Press.

STEDMAN, Carolyn (1982), *The Tidy House*, London: Virago.

STUDY COMMISSION ON THE FAMILY (1981), *Family Finances: An Interim Report From the Working Party on the Financial Circumstances of Families*, London.

TAYLOR, Ian, WALTON, Paul and YOUNG, Jock, (1973), *The New Criminology: For a Social Theory of Deviance*, London: Routledge and Kegan Paul.

THOMAS, W. I. (1907), *Sex and Society*, Boston: Little, Brown and Company.

THORPE, J. and PEASE, K. G. (1976), 'The relationship between recommendations made to the court and sentences passed', *British Journal of Criminology*, vol. 16, no. 4.

UNGERSON, Clare, ed. (1985), *Women and Social Policy*, London: Macmillan.

WALKER, Nigel (1968), *Crime and Punishment in Britain*, Edinburgh; Edinburgh University Press.

WARREN, Marguerite Q., ed. (1981), *Comparing Female and Male Offenders*, Beverly Hills and London: Sage Publications.

WHORF, Benjamin (1956), *Language, Thought and Reality: Selected Writings*, J. Carroll (ed.), Cambridge, Mass: M.I.T. Press.

WHYTE, Judith (1983), *Beyond The Wendy House: Sex Roles In Primary Schools*, London: Longmans.

WILSON, Elizabeth (1977), *Women and The Welfare State*, London: Tavistock.

WOLPE, Anne-Marie (1974), 'The official ideology of education for girls', in Flude and Ahier (eds), op.cit.

WOMEN'S STUDIES GROUP CENTRE FOR CONTEMPORARY CULTURAL STUDIES (1978), *Women Take Issue*, London: Hutchinson.

WORRALL, Anne (1981), 'Out of Place: Female Offenders in Court', *Probation Journal*, vol. 28, no. 3, pp. 90–93.

YOUNG, Michael and WILMOTT, Peter (1962), *Family and Kinship in East London*, Harmondsworth: Penguin.

YOUNG, Michael and WILLMOTT, Peter (1973), *The Symmetrical Family*, London: Routledge and Kegan Paul.

Index